For Russell who, at five years old,

has met many of the people in this book

and without thinking draws parking lots with accessible spaces.

May he and his generation continue to create

a more accessible world.

Disability Today Publishing Group, Inc.
627 Lyons Lane, Suite #203
Oakville, Ontario, Canada L6J 5Z7

Tel: 905.338.6894
Fax: 905.338.1836

Canadian Cataloguing in Publication Data

Portrait of Spirit - One Story At A Time

ISBN 0-9680667-1-2

Printed and bound in Canada

SPECIAL SALES
Portrait of Spirit - One Story At A Time, is available at special discounts for bulk purchases for sales promotions or premiums. For more information, contact Disability Today Publishing Group, Inc.

PORTRAIT OF SPIRIT

ONE STORY AT A TIME

PUBLISHER & EDITOR:
Jeffrey Tiessen

ASSOCIATE EDITOR:
Karen Penner

ART DIRECTION & DESIGN:
Norm Lourenco

PORTRAIT OF SPIRIT

ONE STORY AT A TIME

Text by
MAGGIE HOLTZBERG

Photography by
BILLY HOWARD

Foreword by
CHRISTOPHER REEVE

Published by

Disability Today Publishing Group INC.

ACKNOWLEDGEMENTS

Support from a number of people and organizations made this book possible. They deserve recognition and thanks. Barb Trader, vice president for youth and community services at the Atlanta Paralympic Organizing Committee, was unfailingly supportive. She introduced us to many of the individuals herein. The Georgia Council for the Arts allowed Maggie the time and resources to do the interviews. We are indebted to Jeff Tiessen, our publisher, for sharing our vision and for bringing it to a wider audience.

This book began as a photographic exhibition, which opened in Atlanta during the 1996 Paralympic Games. In an ideal mix of public and private support, the project received funding from Georgia's Office of the Governor, the Louise Staton and Robert Gunn Fund of the Metropolitan Community Foundation, The Jane Smith Turner Foundation, The E.L.A. Foundation, and the Dole Foundation.

Counsel and encouragement came from Alex Aldrich, Moses and Teri Bond, Lucinda Bunnen, Malcolm Call, Will and Kelly Garrett, Caroline Leake, Deborah Lewis, Phillip Rush, Margaret Staton, Raye Varney, Peta Westmas and members of the Cultural Paralympiad Steering Committee.

Above all else, we are grateful to the people you see pictured throughout these pages. They let us into their lives and trusted us to represent themselves to you.

BILLY HOWARD

CONTENTS

—

FOREWORD

In early 1995, I was Christopher Reeve: husband, father, actor, athlete, advocate. Today, I am Christopher Reeve: husband, father, actor, athlete, advocate and person with a disability. My paralysis is part of who I am, but it is only part of who I am.

And so it is with the people in *Portrait of Spirit*. They are mothers, fathers, comedians, administrators, musicians, athletes, lovers — and people with disabilities. They are our friends, our neighbors, our co-workers, members of our communities. While this book opens the door to what it is like to live with a disability, it also shows the diversity of people included in this group.

The people within these pages tell us secrets: how they are treated by others, how children react to them, what it is like to pursue daily life despite physical obstacles. Some of what they have to say may sadden you, but much of it will bring you encouragement and hope.

The importance of Maggie Holtzberg's and Billy Howard's work is the human face it puts on disability. What Holtzberg hears and Howard sees through his lens again and again is the amazing resiliency of the human spirit. One finds oneself looking, not at disabled people, but at individuals with senses, intellects, real lives. While many stories reflect grace and courage, bitterness and anger are represented as well. There is wonderful humor, pathos, and a very clear look at the society in which we all live, but in which disabled persons are often unseen.

As we consider the people we meet through *Portrait of Spirit*, what we must keep in mind is that they are part of us. For better or worse, they are part of the great community that comprises life in these United States. Through their words and portraits, we acknowledge our differences, while celebrating our common ground. People with disabilities are no longer invisible, and many of us have been, and will be, surprised by what we see. As our awareness of the many Americans with disabilities increases, we must come to regard our fellow citizens not with pity, but with understanding. Let's take it one story at a time.

CHRISTOPHER REEVE

INTRODUCTION

This book is about 25 individuals. On the surface, what they have in common is disability. Do they identify themselves first and foremost as being disabled? No. That is something outsiders do. Disability is a social role into which people are cast by the nondisabled community. As Atlanta visual artist David Sampson observed, "I am disabled, handicapped – whatever the current euphemism is at the moment. It seems to have greater bearing on the way others perceive me than it has on my physical reality."

In interviewing the 25 people portrayed in this book, I heard this same basic message over and over again. Paralympic athlete Ann Cody put it this way: "Probably the thing that is most frustrating is that not everybody around me perceives me the same way I perceive me. See, I know what all my challenges are in my life – emotionally, professionally, socially, relationship-wise and everything. All of those things are part of who I am. And my disability is just one cubicle, one cubby-hole of that. So it's frustrating because I have to recognize that when I meet people and when I'm trying to establish relationships or friendships, the disability is always in the forefront of their mind."

This book came about, in part, because 1996 was the year Atlanta hosted the Centennial Olympic Games. Two weeks after the Olympics ended, the city welcomed the Paralympic Games, the ultimate competition for world class, elite athletes with physical disabilities. Many of us were searching for ways in which to heighten awareness of the Paralympic Games and seize the opportunity they offered to change able-bodied people's perceptions of disability. A Cultural Paralympiad was envisioned, the first of its kind.

As it turned out, the public's knowledge of the Paralympic Games, prior to them taking place, was limited. If one mentioned in conversation that the Paralympics were coming to Atlanta, the response often was, "Oh, you mean the Special Olympics?" Though frequently confused, the two are not the same. Whereas the Special Olympics offer a variety of sporting competitions for athletes with mental disabilities (they take place year-round in many different locations) the Paralympic Games are a sporting competition for world-class athletes with physical disabilities held once every four years (since 1960). The Paralympic Games are closely aligned with the Olympic Games.

Paralympic athletes are not people who do well despite their physical limitations; they are people who do well, period. What may come as a surprise to many is that Paralympians finish within seconds of Olympic athletes' results in many events. A double leg amputee has run 100 meters in 11.36 seconds – less than two seconds slower than the current Olympic record. Atlanta's own Al Mead is another such Paralympian. He holds a U.S. record in the high jump at 1.73 meters and set the world record for long jump, winning a gold medal, in the 1988 Seoul Paralympic Games. Four years later, Mead won a silver medal in long jump at the 1992 Barcelona Paralympic Games and sang at the Closing Ceremony. Serving on the Board of Directors of the Atlanta Paralympic Organizing Committee, his was a dedicated voice: "A Paralympian really has a twofold message. One is competition, of course, and going for the gold, but the other is the mission of disabled awareness for all disabled people. In society's eyes, if you're blind, if you're in a wheelchair, if you have an artificial leg, you're disabled. We share that common stigma and that creates a bond among all disabled individuals. That's the beauty with having something like the Paralympics. When you have people jumping as high and as far as they are, in spite of their disability, and running as fast as they do, in spite of their disability, there's a lot to be learned from that."

The remarkable achievement of Paralympic athletes serves as a powerful metaphor for overcoming obstacles. Their "triumph of the human spirit" (the theme slogan for the 1996 Paralympic Games) taps into the great American dream that, with enough hard work, anyone can achieve anything. We may feel moved, inspired and amazed watching Olympic athletes compete. With Paralympic athletes there is that and more. There is a tug at our emotions; what they've overcome is so visible. The flip side of glorifying what some disability rights activists call "super crips" is a subtle suggestion that people with disabilities must strive to be outstanding in order to be worthy. The Games' metaphor of "triumph" may not be as fitting for the 40 million Americans living with disabilities whose day-to-day challenges are less glamorous — hiring attendant care or finding a bus with a wheelchair lift in order to get to work.

Baron Pierre de Coubertin, the father of the modern Olympic movement, said that, "The important thing in the Olympic Games is not to win but to take part. The important thing in life is not the triumph but the struggle." The sentiment is echoed by David Sampson, a visual artist with cerebral palsy, "I don't see myself as triumphing over my disability; it's more like plowing through it."

It was with David Sampson that we began our work. As photographer and folklorist, we set out to gain an insider's perspective. The hope was that nondisabled people would come to know people with disabilities, one story at a time.

Looking back, I feel some obligation to explain why I wanted to interview people with disabilities in the first place. What motivated me, in part, was the recognition of my own discomfort in being around someone using a wheelchair or a white cane. Encounters would feel like playing a game without knowing the rules. How many of us assume that the rules change, just because someone gets around differently? Who among us hasn't entered that awkward dance of misguided attempts to be of help?

So I started talking to people with disabilities. The interviews were tape-recorded and transcribed. They appear here edited down from their original length; some of my questions have been deleted and not all of their words are included. These personal narratives are presented as a distillation, a rendering of the essential self, in much the same way as is each photographic portrait. Everyone has a story, one that, in many cases, has been crafted in the telling over a number of years. These individuals have thought long and hard about how they want to represent themselves to the nondisabled community. If there is a pattern to be discerned in their collective story, it is that they have succinctly reduced their lives to a personal story out of the necessity of defining themselves in a way that most of us do not have to.

This book is not so much about the subject of "the disabled" as it is about the cultural context in which disability occurs. That culture is shaped by the fact that we live in a society which is largely uninvested in the experience of being disabled. Despite the enactment of the Americans with Disabilities Act (ADA), physical and communicative barriers abound. Prejudicial attitudes toward people with disabilities are daunting. Nondisabled adults habitually lump all disabled individuals together. We tend to see the disability first – the limp, the wheelchair, the disfigurement – rather than the person with a disability. We unconsciously assume that life for people with a disability is dismal, and that all people with disabilities think, feel, hurt and react in the same way. In all fairness, this is learned behavior. Just think about how adults react to the natural curiosity of small children encountering someone in a wheelchair, who ask things like, "How come your legs don't work?" "How come that man is sitting in a stroller?" The adult, embarrassed, anxious, hushes the child, "It's not polite to point," or "It's not nice to ask things like that."

As sociologist Irving Kenneth Zola points out, even though the disability – that what makes the person different – is visible and of great interest to children, they are taught to ignore it. "They are not, of course, taught that it is an inconsequential characteristic, but . . . an uncomfortable and all-encompassing one. They are taught to respond globally and not particularistically – to recognize a disabled person when they see one but to ignore the specific characteristics of the (disability)."[†] No wonder able-bodied adults end up "seeing" the disability and not the person. It is like a knee-jerk reaction: we are inspired by the man with cerebral palsy, who is an artist, rather than by the artist, who has cerebral palsy.

Is disability a medical condition or a cultural one? Are people with disabilities part of a cultural group in the way that Italian-Americans, jazz musicians, the Amish or cowboy poets are? Most people who identify themselves as belonging to a cultural group have either grown up in its multi-generational subculture or they have consciously elected to join. Neither is true of the majority of people with disabilities, particularly those who acquire their disability during the course of living. As Mark Johnson put it, 25 years after becoming a quadriplegic, "Being disabled is part of my identity. But I had to get to a place [in my life] to allow it to be part of my identity, because it has such negative connotations. People aren't waiting in line to be disabled."

As for growing up within a subculture John Kemp, President of Very Special Arts, says, "We're different because acquired disabilities aren't passed down from generation to generation. It's not like grandpa telling us about when he was a slave. We don't sit around the fire and hear grandpa tell us what it's like to be an amputee."[††]

Kate Gainer recognizes disability culture but says it is a new phenomenon. "There are things intrinsic about all of us, whether it's an acquired disability or if you were born with it. I think there is an acknowledgment, 'Hey you're one of us. Welcome.' There are certain things, like in other cultures, that we have developed – a certain language that we can use, that other people can't. Like, some of us refer to each other as

[†] Irving Kenneth Zola, "Communication Barriers Between the 'Able-Bodied' and the 'Handicapped'," in *The Psychological and Social Impact of Disability*, edited by Robert P. Marinelli and Arthur E. Ell Orto, New York: Springer Publishing Co., Third Ed., 1991, page 158.

[††] John Kemp, interview in *Enable Magazine*, Summer 1995, page 28.

'crips.' Now that's a no-no if you're able-bodied; you don't say that. But we call each other that."

Establishing a cultural identity as a disabled person requires volition. There is a growing disability rights/independent living movement whose members share a common positive identity based on being disabled. Some of this community's more militant members belong to an organization called ADAPT, which originally stood for American Disabled for Accessible Public Transit. An ADAPT bumper sticker, affixed to the wheelchair of a protester at a recent demonstration, read: "To boldly go where everyone else has been before."

Members of the deaf community, for whom English is a second language, often prefer each other's company to that of someone from the hearing community. Communicating in American Sign Language, the expressive native language of deaf culture, they take pride in their deaf identity. When I asked Robin Titterington if it is true that some members of the deaf community do not consider deafness a disability, her answer was unequivocal. "Oh absolutely. For me here [at work] everyone signs most of the time. I have my TTY, my decoder, my flashing lights."

Remove the barriers and you disinvent disability. Or do you? Billy Golfus, who sustained a brain injury ten years ago says, "The real barriers are the attitudes that see us as sick, incapable, defective, victims of a fate worse than death."★ Emily Cotton, who had a spinal cord injury and has used a wheelchair for 15 years, smiles when I ask her about how able-bodied people perceive people with disabilities. "Sometimes they think that maybe you have some kind of illness and they don't want to touch you," she said. The fact is, most people with disabilities are not sick. For example, someone born with cerebral palsy has a permanent neurological disorder, not a disease.

Historically, the general public's perceptions of disabled people have been greatly influenced by the medical model of disability ("the disabled" as damaged goods). Loss of hearing, severed spinal cords and atrophied limbs are perceived as pathological conditions limiting what a person can do. These perceptions, these projections of incapability, have the effect of being just as restrictive as concrete sidewalks without curb-cuts. Assistant Secretary of Education Judy Heumann asserts, "Neither the wheelchair nor my disability is the problem. The problem is the lack of physical access. The problem is people's perceptions of what I can or can't do. That becomes a part of my reality, because their beliefs in what I can or cannot do really affect what they allow me to do."★★

Unless you or someone close to you has a disability, or unless, through writing a grant or constructing a building you are compelled to meet ADA accessibility requirements, chances are you may not have given much thought to the experience of being disabled. And without thought, it is far too easy to sentimentalize the lives of people with disabilities, to portray them as either shining examples of inspiration or pitiable victims of tragic circumstances. Realistically, the majority of people who live with disabilities occupy the middle ground between triumph and despair. *Portrait of Spirit* is largely about capturing that middle ground.

MAGGIE HOLTZBERG

★   Billy Golfus, *When Billy Broke His Head . . . And Other Tales of Wonder*, a film by Billy Golfus and David Simpson, National Disability Awareness Project, 1994.

★★ Timothy J. McNulty, "Advocates for disabled troubled by GOP challenges to laws," *The Atlanta Journal/Constitution*, February 19, 1995, page C4.

"I USUALLY SAY I GOT STARTED MAKING ART BECAUSE I COULDN'T CLIMB TREES."

DAVID SAMPSON

Artist

David Sampson is a painter, sculptor, and a man of keen wit and intelligence. His gift for expressiveness in visual forms has brought him recognition in the art world. Having cerebral palsy affects his voluntary motor skills and his speech. He says his fast forward is most people's slow motion.

I am a painter and sculptor. One of the earliest influences on me was Toulouse Latrec. I remember in particular a wine glass, which he rendered with maybe four strokes. I don't remember the painting it was in, but what struck me was that he captured the essence of something with minimal strokes. I saw it as the visual equivalent of my physical need to be verbally concise – because of the physical effort of talking.

My memory of it is that those four strokes didn't necessarily touch each other. I think in seeking to paint the essence of the subject rather than the details leaves the viewer free to interject their own interpretation into the piece. I think if a work of art can be said to have a life of its own, it's because there is a dialogue between the viewer and the piece.

WAS BEING AN ARTIST SOMETHING YOU KNEW YOU WANTED TO PURSUE VERY EARLY ON?

At its earliest point, it might have been more a matter of not knowing anything else to do.

At some point it switched to wanting to be an artist. Although, I certainly didn't have a clue as to what that meant.

WHAT DOES IT MEAN TO YOU NOW TO BE AN ARTIST?

In which voice, the positive or the cynical? The first word that comes to mind is 'prostitute' because you're always selling yourself. Whether it's being out there physically or hiding behind the canvas, it is somewhat the same. Frequently, to make a living at it, it's selling yourself by doing something you would rather not be doing.

In many ways, I think being an artist is more a lifestyle than a career. It's not something I pick up in the morning and put down at five o'clock. It's a way of living, thinking and perceiving the world around me. And it's because I perceive the world around me the way I do, I create the work I create. If I could turn it off, sometimes I think I would.

HOW DOES THE NATURE OF YOUR DISABILITY AFFECT YOUR WORK?

There are times when I can lose myself in the work. Then there are other times when getting my hand to do anything I want is sheer agony. Over the years my physical dexterity has changed. Fortunately, the kind of images I want to produce seems to change just before or simultaneously with the physical change. Generally speaking, I'm not physically painting today as I did ten years ago. And I'm not making the same kind of images as I did ten years ago. Each affects the other.

Cerebral palsy can manifest itself in a wide variety of physical situations. In my case, it affects my voluntary motor skills over which I have little control, or in some cases, no control. And the voluntary motion that I can make requires much concentration. I have to think about getting my tongue to move the way it's moving to make the sounds it's currently making. I actually think about moving my hand to pick up the sandwich, to get it from the plate to my mouth and then back to the plate again.

The degree to which I am aware of the concentration needed varies from day to day and sometimes from minute to minute. Stress is a very strong indicator. With mental or physical stress, my dexterity goes out the window and I become physically tired. Being cold affects muscle tone, which affects dexterity. Alcohol is another factor. A little bit of alcohol can make speaking easier but there's a fine line which once crossed makes things infinitely more difficult.

DO YOU THINK OF YOURSELF AS DISABLED?

Within the context of the environment that I've created for myself, I'm certainly aware that at times I am severely inconvenienced. Ordinarily, activities which would take you 15 minutes to accomplish can frequently take me an hour to do. In that context, I'm acutely aware of being inconvenienced.

I'm 'disabled', 'handicapped' – whatever the current euphemism is at the moment. But that does seem to have a greater bearing on the way others perceive me than it has on my own physical reality. There are obviously people who look at someone who is in a wheelchair and immediately think that individual is confined to that chair – never perceiving the individual separate from, or out of, the apparatus that's being used for transportation.

Yet then there are other people that are intuitively different. They perceive the inner person free from the exterior constraints. And I expect, for those people who are able to do that, their ability to do that doesn't begin and end with me. I'm sure they perceive everyone they meet the same way.

I suspect that my speech tends to be far more off-putting to a far wider variety of individuals, than does my sitting in a wheelchair. After all, a paraplegic sits in a wheelchair. A paraplegic behind a desk with 'normal' speech patterns and 'normal' physical dexterity could suddenly be perceived as a 'normal' human being.

There is also the subconscious, psychological advantage the paraplegic has in that the medical technology, which enabled spinal cord injured people to survive their injury, came out of war-time medicine. The first paraplegics seen in society were all war veterans giving the subconscious connection between paraplegics and honorable war veterans.

There is a very definite pecking order of disability. This order stems from society's perspective of disabled people. The bottom line is, the more obviously different from the norm you are, the more fear is associated with that difference. Someone with my extent of cerebral palsy is far down in the order. Both our speech as well as our physical movement are definitely very different from the norm. You just can't sit us at a desk and perceive us as ordinary.

IF THERE WAS A YOUNG PERSON WHO HAD CEREBRAL PALSY WHO WANTED TO BE AN ARTIST, WHAT WOULD YOU TELL HIM OR HER?

Assuming this person is in his or her late teens or older, I would say the same thing I would say to anybody interested in being an artist, regardless of whether they had a disability or not. I'd say, 'Ask yourself a question. Is this something you have to do or something you want to do. If the answer is something you have to do, pursue it full steam ahead. Give it everything you've got. If it's something you want to do, take classes, enjoy it, have fun with it. Have a great time with it but find yourself an easier way to make a living.' ♣

"I RECENTLY DIVORCED; IT'S JUST BEEN A YEAR. I TELL PEOPLE THAT IF GOD WAS STANDING IN FRONT OF ME AND SAID, 'EMILY, I'M GOING TO GIVE YOU A CHOICE. I'M GOING TO LET YOU PICK A SPINAL CORD INJURY OR A DIVORCE,' I WOULD SAY, 'I'LL TAKE THE SPINAL CORD INJURY, 50 TIMES OVER THE DIVORCE.'"

EMILY COTTON

Wheelchair Saleswoman for National Seating and Mobility

Emily Cotton refers to the violent attempt on her life fourteen years ago as "one of those stories you read about" in the newspaper. The act left her paralyzed. Rehabilitation professionals did not waste much time before telling her she would never walk again. Six weeks after her injury, Cotton became involved with wheelchair sports and is now a competitive water skier. In addition to her work as a saleswoman, Cotton does peer support at the Shepherd Center, an Atlanta-based rehabilitation facility, to help patients realize that there is life after rehabilitation. In her own estimation, she is healthier now than before her injury.

I'm a T-7 paraplegic, injured as a result of a gun shot wound December 15, 1981. I was shot at work, sitting in my car, by my ex-husband. We were estranged at the time. He shot me five times, point blank, with a .38 caliber hand gun. One of the bullets severed my spinal cord and left me a paraplegic. He left the scene of the 'accident' and shot himself in the head. I wasn't told that he had died for about three days. People look at me and say, "God, weren't you mad? Aren't you angry?" When someone's dead, it's really hard to hold onto that anger. To me it's a fruitless expense of energy to be angry at someone for years.

One of the first things you realize after rehab is, 'God, I can wear something besides sweatpants.' With a spinal cord injury, you do your rehab and you either get it together or you don't. But you move on. As far as depression, I was much more depressed throughout my divorce [from my second husband] than I was after my spinal cord injury. The emotional pain that you feel in a divorce is so much different than a traumatic injury. With spinal cord injury, you have all these people that are up, that are trying to help you. You have PTs (physiotherapists); you have OTs (occupational therapists); you have all these people saying, "You're going to be OK." They're trying to keep you busy. They're supporting you and they're taking you out. In divorce, nobody even wants to be around you! It's like, "She's miserable. She's going to bite my head off, she's going to cry."

THE WHOLE AREA OF HOW ABLE-BODIED PEOPLE PERCEIVE SOMEONE WITH A DISABILITY ... WHAT KIND OF ASSUMPTIONS DO PEOPLE MAKE?

I basically grew up in the South but I was on the West Coast for eight years where I noticed that people's attitudes are much different, much more open. In the South, what you see a lot of is, people patting us on the head. It is very evident when people are condescending. Or they feel sorry for you or they go out of their way to help you. Sometimes they think you're sick and that maybe you have some kind of illness and they don't want to touch you. One of the most common things, and it happens to all of us, is when you may be sitting in a movie line or a food line and someone comes up to you and says something like, "I want you to know that I was in a wheelchair one time. I had an accident. The doctors told me that I would never walk again. But look! I'm up walking. You just have to believe that you'll walk again."

I think that that kind of attitude towards miracles or God and religion is probably much more prevalent in the South than it is on the West Coast. I've had women come up to me in New Orleans and invite me to a healing. I was there for a road race but they wanted me to come to a healing. Most of us are well enough adjusted that we just go, "Well thank you," turn away and laugh it off. You try to be polite most of the time.

DO PEOPLE GENERALLY UNDERESTIMATE WHAT YOU CAN DO?

A great deal. And I think that we sometimes feel that we need to over-achieve or over-compensate. Maybe it takes us a little longer to do a task or we need some assistance with it, so we may go out of our way to make up for an inadequacy or an inability to do something.

I had an appointment this morning with a client that has cerebral palsy. Liz, the therapist I've been working together with for several years now, was there. I'm wheeling up the driveway and it's very steep. I get to the house and the girl's mom says, "Well, Liz didn't tell me you were in a wheelchair." Liz looked at her and she started laughing and she said, "Well you know, I didn't even think about it." When you're involved in relationships with people, it's wonderful when they get to that point where your disability doesn't even register with them anymore. You're a person, whether you have a disability or not. They completely forget that you're mobility impaired and use a wheelchair.

One of the most enlightening things that I've come up with is this: 'deep down you're the same person that you were before your disability. It doesn't change you. It doesn't make you different. If you were angry, if you were lazy, if you were a pig, you are probably still going to be that way.' ♣

"BEING DISABLED IS PART OF MY IDENTITY. BUT I HAD TO GET TO A PLACE TO ALLOW IT TO BE PART OF MY IDENTITY, BECAUSE IT HAS SUCH NEGATIVE CONNOTATIONS. PEOPLE AREN'T WAITING IN LINE TO BE DISABLED."

MARK JOHNSON

Advocate, Shepherd Center

Ten years after sustaining a cervical neck injury which resulted in quadriplegia, Mark Johnson became involved with ADAPT, the disability rights group that made a priority out of equipping city buses with wheelchair lifts in the 1980s. Johnson has such an uncanny charisma that his confrontational edge comes as a surprise. It is a winning combination for this civil rights activist who has led dozens of protests on government property.

I was a sophomore in college in 1971. One night, a bunch of us decided to go out to a quarry that we had been swimming in for years – diving off the cliffs really. That night I hit the bottom. One of the guys I was swimming with noticed I wasn't moving and grabbed me.

All of a sudden I was a person with a disability and the image I had of disability was twofold: the veteran on the skateboard on the street corner and grandma with a blanket over her legs. Those were my images of disability 25 years ago. Expectations changed. The expectation was no longer that you'd have relationships again or that you might actually get married or have a family or live on your own. The prevalent attitude was best paraphrased by what my parents were told by staff at the rehab center: "He'll always be this way. Take him home. Take good care of him and when y'all die put him in a nursing home." It was that crazy aunt in the basement syndrome – "let's hide 'em, you know, not let 'em out."

How have things changed?

In the old days, a person with my level of injury would come to a place like this [Shepherd Center] for five months. With today's health care reform, people are not here very long anymore. About a year ago, average hospitalization here went down to 100 days and now it's headed down to 70 days. People are turned around here fast now. You're still trying to figure out what happened, what the impact is going to be, how you're going to (use the bathroom) and then all of a sudden you're out of here. You may have been lucky enough to go on one outing for a couple of hours where you experienced people staring or gawking. But you haven't had time to internalize how to deal with it. In the past, you'd be here long enough to talk about how to deal with it.

How did you become such an advocate for change?

I needed to get to a point where I could say, 'My disability is just part of who I am. It's part of my identity.' That's a transition that occurs. I had to accept the fact that I was different. Then I had to get to the point where I was saying, 'I'm not going to be treated differently just because I'm different.' But nobody ever teaches you how to rock the boat. I never went to a class in school on how to create change.

I started support groups in '77. Those support groups were good but you got tired of going to bitch, moan and groan sessions. I wanted to get on with life. So a group of us started doing things to make a difference. We started changing building codes. If money was allocated to build a recreation center then we wanted to be able to use that rec center too. But I hadn't ever participated in direct action civil disobedience because I just didn't think you had to do that in this society. 'Me, have to do that? Give me a break.'

What really turned the corner for me was realizing there was no legal requirement to make express buses accessible. I was a taxpayer and that taxpaying money was buying vehicles that I couldn't use. I started believing, like a lot of other people, that I was a member of the public and I wanted to use public transit. Rosa Parks wanted to sit anywhere on the bus; I just wanted to get on. We planned demonstrations in Colorado in '81 and '82. I was a new, naive, good-looking 'white boy' they could stick up on the front line. We won the battle in Colorado for all buses to be lift-equipped, not just the ones on fixed routes.

By '83, people around the country were calling us saying, "You won, can you help us?" In '84 we started looking for the root of the problem. It was the American Public Transit Association and we went after them. Someone came up with the name ADAPT – American Disabled for Accessible Public Transit. We won battles from '84 to '89. The last action was in Atlanta where we occupied a federal building and spent the night there. People were dragged out. Then we decided we'd kick off a new campaign for attendant services and that's when ADAPT became American Disabled for Attendant Programs Today. We were trying to teach people new tactics. We were trying to counter the telethon mentality. ♣

> "I GREW UP IN A CHRISTIAN HOME SO WHEN I WAS TOLD THAT MY LEG WOULD BE AMPUTATED, IT DIDN'T REALLY AFFECT ME LIKE YOU THINK IT WOULD, BECAUSE I THOUGHT GOD WOULD GROW IT BACK."

AL MEAD

Paralympic Medalist, Track and Field

As a youngster, Al Mead lost his left leg above the knee due to circulatory problems. Mead has grown into the quintessential Paralympic athlete, whose excellence in competitive sport is equalled only by his commitment to increased awareness of the abilities of persons with a disability. He holds a U.S. high jump record at 1.73 meters. He set the world record for the long jump with a gold medal performance in the 1988 Paralympic Games in Seoul, Korea. Four years later in Barcelona, Mead won a silver medal in the long jump and sang at the closing ceremony. Due to an injury, Mead failed to qualify to compete in the 1996 Paralympic Games in Atlanta. In addition to his athletic life, Mead is vice president of an executive search firm.

I was a pretty active kid, a fast kid. I was always running and playing. At recess time, when the bell would ring, we would all run across the parking lot – this big chasm between the swings and the door. I would always be the first one to the door. When my leg was amputated that changed things.

The blood circulation had stopped in my left leg. Doctors determined that they had to amputate it so the infection would not spread. I was nine years old.

When I came home from the hospital with one leg, reality did set in. I can specifically remember sitting on a fire hydrant on the corner of the block where we lived. I was just sitting, relaxing and enjoying things while everybody was in school. Cars eventually started stopping and one person got out. That person felt sorry for me and started giving me some money. Right then I knew that I didn't want to be known as some sorry, benevolent case. At that point I believe I really turned things around.

Sports was a rehabilitation tool for me to get back into the mainstream of life. I wasn't in any type of structured rehabilitation program. Primarily, it was just me in my neighborhood. It was like on-the-

job training. But in sports, there is an arena where you get respect when you are competitive.

WERE YOU EVER SELF-CONSCIOUS ABOUT YOUR PROSTHESIS?

You're talking about a kid who had to endure walking down the hallway with a squeaky leg or a loose foot. Kids would actually laugh; it would hurt me. Back then prostheses were very ancient. Technology has brought prosthetics a long way, but back then a wooden leg was truly a wooden leg. Bolts, belts, the whole shebang. Before me, my prosthetist never had had anyone so active and who broke his leg all the time from jumping off fences and swings, or playing basketball and baseball so hard. I broke my feet all the time. Ball bearings were always all over the floor.

So I was faced with a dilemma. Either I'd stop doing sports so I would have a decent working leg or I would continue on and just deal with the fact that I was going to have a raggedy-looking leg because I was pushing it so hard.

I never showed my artificial leg to anyone until high school, believe it or not. From third grade to high school I never wore shorts in public because I had this thing about already getting a lot of attention. More attention would just be overbearing. I always wore sweatpants. I was still figuring out who the heck I was. What was I going to be? My ambition was to be competitive in sports.

I think everything finally came together when I started competing against other disabled people who were as competitive as I was. All of a sudden I had a group of people I could lean on and be a part of because they were athletes as well. I competed in my first track and field meet in 1982 and broke the 200 meter world record for my disability classification. In 1984 I set the 100 meter world record which stood for about six years. At the 1988 Paralympics in Seoul, Korea, I won a gold medal, breaking the world record in the long jump.

Technology also played a part. I now have the latest in technology in my new prosthesis, which is strictly for competition. I used to run with a hop-skip method. That was the common way for an above-the-knee amputee to run. This new leg allows me to run step-over-step in a regular stride.

DO YOU FEEL A COMMON IDENTITY WITH OTHER PEOPLE WITH DISABILITIES?

Absolutely. There's definitely a common identity because in society's eyes if you're blind, if you use a wheelchair, if you have an artificial leg, then you're "disabled". And so, we share that common stigma and that creates a bond among all disabled individuals. ♣

AL MEAD

"THE FIRST TIME ROBERT EVER SAID ANYTHING ABOUT MY HAVING NO LEGS WAS WHEN HE WAS ABOUT FOUR YEARS OLD. FOUR OR FIVE. WE WERE TAKING A SHOWER TOGETHER. AND HE EXPRESSED SOME SADNESS THAT I HAD LOST MY LEGS. I THINK HE STARTED CRYING AND JUST SAID, 'I WISH YOU HADN'T LOST YOUR LEGS.' THEN HE GAVE ME A HUG. GOD, THAT BROKE MY HEART."

RODGER CARROLL

Father, Vietnam War Veteran

Rodger Carroll was 19 when he volunteered for the service. The Vietnam War cost him his legs. Nearly 30 years later, Carroll leads a fulfilling life – he is as passionate about his study of the Greek Classics as he is about perfecting his golf game. A refreshing mix of sensitivity and machismo, he gets choked up telling the story of his son's birth, his visit to the Vietnam Memorial, or his son's first signs of empathy toward his wounded body.

When I first got out of the service, most people that knew me before thought, "Oh my God, his life is ended". But that's just not true. It was a new beginning. That's how I looked at it.

I volunteered for the service. I think when you're nineteen you do a lot of crazy things. That was one of them. But I have no regrets about it. I think it made me a better person.

CAN YOU TELL ME HOW YOU BECAME A DOUBLE LEG AMPUTEE?

I was in Vietnam for seven or eight weeks. I was in a paratrooper unit. It was in the 173rd Airborne and we were stationed at Benwah Airbase, which was next to a supply depot. Our unit was in a fire fight about 20 miles north of Saigon. The F.O. – the forward observer – started calling in artillery around the outside of our position. One of the rounds fell short. We got wounded by our own artillery. It happened a lot. I was the most severely wounded soldier that survived. It killed a boy who was further away from the blast than I was. So I was very fortunate.

My right foot was blown off completely. When I looked down, I could just see the stump of my

leg. My right boot and foot were nearby – smoking. My left knee was gone. My whole knee was gone. The kneecap was hanging. I was looking down on my kneecap and it was just a huge hole there.

I was conscious the whole time. I felt nothing; I was absolutely numb. No pain whatsoever. They were always warning us, try to stay as calm as you can if you're wounded. There were guys all around us. Unfortunately there was a lot of fire going around us. The fight ended about ten minutes after I was wounded, I guess. I remember saying to myself, 'I don't want to go into shock; just don't go into shock; shock can kill you.' When they were able to get to me I told them, 'Don't let me go into shock. Stay here and talk to me.' They did. If it had been in any other war I would have been dead. People have no idea how bad war is. The damage to the human body that you can suffer and still stay alive is just incredible.

You don't talk about this much, do you?

Well ... no I don't. If anybody asks me about it I'll talk about it. There's so much pain involved in seeing people dying. Someone who has not been through a war can't understand what it's like.

When I first came back, that's all I did. It was on my mind constantly. I talked and talked and talked and talked and talked. But everybody talked about the war then, it was 1967. "What was it like?" "What happened to you?" "Why were you there?" I did a lot of talking about it and a lot of thinking about it. But now when I think about the war, I have more of a sense of sadness – the waste that went on there. And when I think of those 18 and 19-year-old kids ... I mean, I spent my 20th birthday in the hospital.

I started back to school about two years after I got back. I was 22. It was there that I started doing some big thinking about Vietnam – how I got there, mostly. I realized that I was raised to think about how men were supposed to be. I never really had the opportunity to think outside of those categories. I hate to say it but, I wasn't a very reflective, sensitive human being. They don't want sensitive men in the paratroopers, okay!

I started thinking about how I got there, rather than what happened to me, and I started understanding what role my family had in it, what role my culture had in it. What saved me was that I eventually had to assume some responsibility for what happened. I had to say that I signed the papers. I got on a helicopter. I picked up the gun. And although I was 19 and didn't know that much about it, didn't want to go on that helicopter and didn't want to go out in that jungle, I did anyway. I assumed responsibility for it and that freed me. Saying, 'I did it' was an incredibly freeing experience. I signed the papers and I went – not because of Lyndon Johnson, or Dean Rusk, or anyone's policy, or the American consciousness of the 1950s and '60s.

My son Robert, my wife Suzette and I went up to Washington recently. I'd been there before but I'd never been to the Wall. I looked up one of the boy's names. I was going to look them all up – all of the guys that I knew over there that were killed. But I couldn't. I just couldn't. I just saw this guy's name – Josefeld Duckett. Duckett, that's what I always called him. You didn't know first names in the army. He was from Washington, D.C. and was always accusing me of being a hillbilly. He was killed over there. I didn't know seeing his name would affect me as much as it did. I had to go sit down. We were planning to go over to the Lincoln Memorial but I couldn't. I just got a taxi and went back to the hotel.

DID YOUR SON UNDERSTAND?

Oh yeah. He said, "Now what's so special about this guy dad?" I told Robert that he was killed the day I was wounded. He got real quiet. I never miss an opportunity to tell Robert how crazy war is. What you're playing is a game. But how can you explain war to a little boy? You can't.

YOUNG CHILDREN USUALLY ASK QUESTIONS WHEN THEY NOTICE SOMEONE IN A WHEELCHAIR. DO YOU HAVE ANY MEMORIES ABOUT HOW ROBERT REACTED?

Most kids, up to two or three years old, don't care whether you're in a wheelchair or not. For any child that has ever asked me a question about it, I am more than willing to answer them. They are just curious and want to talk about it.

I remember this one little boy who came over to spend the night. I had my legs on but then got off my legs and got into my wheelchair. I don't think this boy ever realized I had two artificial legs. And I can remember when I went in to give Robert a hug goodnight. As I went out, I heard his friend say, "Boy, Robert, your father is really weird." But Robert doesn't seem to be very self-conscious about it at all. One day he came home and said, "Can I take your bronze star in to show the kids?" I said sure. The biggest compliment that I can get from Robert is to see that he's proud of me. If Robert loves me as much as I love my father, I'll consider myself successful as a person.

WHEN DO YOU USE YOUR LIMBS AND WHEN DO YOU USE A WHEELCHAIR?

I use my legs whenever I go out of the house, as much as possible. I mean, I would never go out of the house in a wheelchair, just because of the barriers. It's a lot harder to get around in a wheelchair than it is on two legs, even with two artificial legs.

SO WHAT'S THE MOST DIFFICULT THING ABOUT —

... most difficult thing about my legs? Hitting a golf ball consistently is the most difficult thing I've done. I'm serious.

I don't mind talking about disability but you ask me questions about it as if it dominates my life. And it doesn't. I think issues of disability are just so small compared to some of the big things in life, like our children. I'd *much* rather talk about that. ♣

RODGER CARROLL

"THERE ARE A LOT OF JOKES ABOUT THE WAR, BLACK HUMOR. A FRIEND OF MINE, HE'S SHOT, SAME LIKE I AM. AND HE'S DISABLED. HE SAID, 'YOU KNOW WHAT, IZZIE? BEFORE WAR, BEFORE I GOT SHOT, PEOPLE, MY FRIENDS, THEY CARRY ME FROM BAR, OUTSIDE. NOW THEY MUST TO CARRY ME IN BAR, INSIDE.'"

ISMET OMERASEVIC

Engineer and President, Bosnian-American Cultural Association

Having come to the United States in the mid-1980s as an engineer, Ismet Omerasevic felt compelled to return to Bosnia to defend his country. He joined a combat unit and in 1992 was hit by Serbian fire, which paralyzed him from the waist down. Asked to describe the Bosnian character in one word he chooses, "Merhamet," meaning "generosity." He hopes to help Bosnian Americans be better countrymen by remembering their Bosnian culture.

I am born and raised in Bosnia, 80 miles north of Sarejevo. Sarejevo is an Olympic city. 1984 was Winter Olympic Games in Sarejevo. But now there is nothing left from the Olympics. Everything destroyed.

I was a soldier. I was comandeered in some unit in Bosnia. I defend my country, my birthplace, from Serbian aggressors. So in fight I got shot by Serbs. Bullet goes through right lung and hits spine. From that day, this was September 8th, 1992, I am paralyzed from waist down. So that's natural, from war. You see, I've been in front line. When I got shot I have four or five of my fellow soldiers near to me and they take me from fire line to hospital, which was 30 miles from that place. There is no transportation; they carry me by hand. Over hills, over mountains because there is war.

You see, life goes on. You must think about your family. About kids. I don't have time to think about me. I must raise my kids and I must educate my kids which keeps you to go on. See I was, personally, a happy person. I like jokes – that's what keeps me alive. So, still happy. I say I have plus now because I don't need to spend money on shoes. Who needs shoes?

For us, United States is not new country because we already spent six years here. I was plant manager at a furniture manufacturer in Houston, Texas for six years. When war broke out I said, 'There is my country, there is my family, so I cannot stay here and watch what's happening over there. I must to go over there to see maybe I can help.'

In Bosnia, buildings and public places are not made for disabled people. Here, you have access for disabled people. There, if you cannot walk, someone must carry you. That's a problem. But I think, after this war, Bosnian government must do same things like here, because a lot of people are disabled.

See I have one joke. I was in middle of offensive action with Serbs. And my comrade, he was with me behind the barrier. I see him there searching down there on the ground. I said, 'What are you doing?' Blood is everywhere. He said, "I got shot, my ear." Sniper has shot his ear. I said, 'Forget it.' He said, "I can forget here [pointing to his head] but my cigarette was behind my ear." He will forget ear, but cigarette he will not forget.

I've been involved in war. You see, country, your own country, is like spirit, your own spirit; if you don't have country you don't have spirit. So, you must be there, try to help. ♣

ROBIN J. TITTERINGTON

Director, Georgia Interpreting Services Network

Born with spina bifida, Robin Titterington says she was mainstreamed long before it was ever called mainstreaming. During her freshman year in college she lost her hearing due to a side effect from the medication she was taking following kidney surgery. When she took a semester off to learn sign language and lip reading at Gallaudet University in Washington, D.C., a close friend bemoaned the fact that she was going off to "read Yankee lips". Robin graduated with honors and went on to become the first director of Georgia's Interpreting Services Network.

Back in 1973 there were not a lot of options for where people in wheelchairs could go to school. St. Andrews was the first place where I saw a real wheelchair ramp. After my freshman year there, I lost my hearing. St. Andrews was wonderful for people in wheelchairs, but not great for deaf people. After a year and a half, I went to Gallaudet University for one semester. Gallaudet, at that time, was wonderful for deaf people, but really lousy for people in wheelchairs. I couldn't even get out of my dorm by myself. But the people at Gallaudet were wonderful. They would introduce me and say, "This is Robin. She's new deaf. Sign slow."

People have said to me, "You're not really deaf." I'm not the same kind of deaf as somebody who was born deaf but that does not make me less deaf. It almost seems like they're trivializing what I went through when I became deaf, which was not easy. Not all deaf people are the same. Deafness is more of a cultural identity than a medical one. I have a button that says, "Proud to be Deaf." I'm sure a lot of people wouldn't understand that. We still hear stories about deaf kids who think they

are going to become hearing when they grow up, or that they're going to die when they grow up because they don't see any deaf adults.

For some late-deafened adults it's still very hard for them to say they are deaf. I think it's hard because it is invisible. A good friend of mine, who signs very well, will sign when he is with interpreters but when he goes into a store he tells people he is hard of hearing. He's not hard of hearing – he's as deaf as that desk! He says that people give him very weird looks and bad attitudes if he uses the word "deaf." I use it all the time. I'll say, 'I'm deaf. I need to read your lips.'

THERE ARE A NUMBER OF WAYS DEAF PEOPLE COMMUNICATE WITH EACH OTHER AND WITH HEARING PEOPLE, RIGHT?

American Sign Language is what deaf people who grew up deaf usually use. Its grammar is very different from English. You really can't use your voice and sign American Sign Language at the same time. The word order is different. You use a lot more expression and often things are acted out. It takes a lot of different skills – perception, translation, hand coordination and memory – to be a good signer. It's a beautiful language.

DOES SOMEONE WHO WANTS TO BE AN INTERPRETER HAVE TO HAVE THOSE SKILLS AS WELL?

A good signer and a good interpreter are two different things. A good interpreter obviously has to be fluent in both languages and they need to perceive, translate, move their hands and remember. If you ask deaf people about interpreters, the most important thing to them is confidentiality. Keeping your mouth shut. That's very important. If an interpreter came in here and interpreted for a little bit, tomorrow he or she couldn't tell somebody, "Yeah, I interpreted for Robin and Maggie." That's for us to tell if we want to tell somebody. It sounds like nothing – maybe he interpreted for me at the dentist. That's not a big deal. But who is he to decide if that's nothing? It's up to the deaf person to tell if they want it known.

WHAT KINDS OF OBSTACLES MAKE IT HARDER FOR YOU TO UNDERSTAND PEOPLE?

Accents are really hard. And most deaf people would say that. Interestingly, I understand Northerners much better. But most people I know are the opposite – they understand Southerners better. It's funny because Northerners speak so fast. I usually understand women better than men. Some people just mumble; some people always have their hands in front of their mouths.

Being creative with language helps. My mom, she's very good. She'll say, "How's your car?" And I'll say, 'What?' She'll come back with, "How's your automobile; how's your Honda?" She'll find something I can hear. My brothers on the other hand will say, "How's your car?" 'What?' "How's your car?" 'What?' "How's your car?"

I never have a problem with children. I give them what they ask. I try not to go into a lot of explanation if they don't ask for it. "Why are you in the chair?" 'I can't walk.' If they ask more I tell them more. Children are wonderful. It's the parents I have a problem with. They yank the kids away. I'm on my second generation of nieces and nephews and when I go to visit they say, "Get out of the chair Aunt Robin, I want to roll."

Reading lips. It's so 'iffy'. You can make a bad mistake and look really stupid. I have a funny story

ROBIN J. TITTERINGTON

from a couple of months ago. I was talking with Bryant and Beth – my co-workers – and we were trying to figure out something about interpreting in foster care. Bryant and I didn't know anything about that program and I said, 'Beth, do you know anything about foster care?' She doesn't sign much and said something like, "Oh yes, my best friend, whom I will love until I die, was in foster care." But she signed about three words out of that whole sentence. And I said, 'What? You're best friend to die? What?' And Bryant started laughing and Beth was looking kind of hurt. So she said it again and I still didn't get it. I said something like, 'You're best friend wants you to die?' Bryant was now really laughing and Beth was really confused. Finally I started saying every word I understood as she talked. I kept missing the word "until." Eventually, I got it. I said, 'Okay, time for deaf awareness.' When you're taught lip reading you're taught to say the part of the sentence you understood so the hearing person will know what you missed. So I said to Bryant and Beth, 'Sometimes we look kind of dumb, but that's okay because I know you love me, right?' And Bryant said, "Until I die." ❧

PHIL RUSSELL GREEN

Fly Fisherman

When Phil Green began having trouble driving back in 1978, he went to see his doctor. He was diagnosed with retinitis pigmentosa. The disease manifests itself through the clumping of pigment on the retina. Eyesight diminishes in concentric patterns, eventually resulting in total blindness. Green works at the Center for Disease Control in Atlanta.

I've always fished. I can't see the fly once it gets past twenty or thirty feet. I'm essentially waiting to feel a strike of a fish. It's something that I have a great deal of control over. That's the key, having control over things in your life. Everyone wants to feel that.

If I'm not looking directly at something, I don't see it. In a low light or crowded situation I may stumble. Or, I may not see that someone has their hand out to shake. I may not see that someone just walked away and I may end up talking to thin air. In many situations it's not perceivable that there is anything wrong with my sight. During daylight hours I can still get around without the use of a cane but at night that's impossible. Part of the disease is the inability to see at night. Early on, people might perceive that I had been drinking because I would miss steps or stumble or bump into people. I guess they still do. But I can't go through life apologizing every time I bump into something.

When the employers I had in Fort Worth, Texas found out that I had this disease, they fired me. I was a health, restaurant and food manufacturing plant inspector and the job entailed driving. At that time no one could conceive of there being anything else that I could do. At that time, the Rehabilitation Act of 1973 had just come into effect, but had no teeth. It didn't have any teeth until the Americans with Disabilities Act was passed in 1990.

Of all the different disability groups, the blind probably suffer the highest rate of unemployment. I've been fortunate in that I've always been able to find a job. Now if I were totally blind, or in a wheelchair, it might be a different story. I've worked for the government and they tend to have a more active role in hiring people with different impairments. But I guess you only want to have just enough. I've worked places where people have been blind, have been in wheelchairs or on crutches or have been deaf, but none of them have been in management ... unless they're already there and then an accommodation is made because of years of service.

ASIDE FROM THE OBVIOUS, HOW DO YOU THINK A VISUAL IMPAIRMENT – ESPECIALLY ONE THAT OCCURS GRADUALLY – DIFFERS FROM OTHER DISABILITIES?

When losing your sight, you're losing something that's so integral to our species. Our entire society is visually oriented. And there's a misconception about blind people in general. There are all these expressions in our culture that connect the fact that you can't see something to a defective brain or soul ... things like, "So-and-so's blind as a bat" or "they can't see their nose in front of their face." Even in our literature you'll find a lot of references to not being able to see used in different metaphors relating to the soul or to the heart. Probably if there were more blind people, things would be a whole lot different. ♣

PHIL RUSSELL GREEN

"IF I DIED TODAY, I WOULD SAY I HAVE HAD ONE HELL OF A TIME. I HAVE LAUGHED MORE THAN MY SHARE AND CERTAINLY LOVED MORE THAN MY SHARE. IT'S ALMOST LIKE LIFE IS THIS BIG PARTY THAT I'VE BEEN INVITED TO AND I'M JUST HAVING A HELL OF A TIME. AND I AIN'T LEAVING 'TIL IT'S DARK."

TOMMY FUTCH

Improvisational Comedian

Tommy Futch exudes creativity. He is the artistic leader of Laughing Matters, an improvisational comedy group that has been in existence since 1985. A 1971 car wreck that paralyzed him was not the only catastrophe in his seventeenth year. Soon after he lost the use of his legs, his mother died. Eventually, he left his Deep South rural roots for the big city.

I grew up in tiny Nashville, Georgia. In the daytime it's gnats, at night it's mosquitoes. And it's humidity, 24 hours a day. I was the second person in a wheelchair, in my town – except for old people. The first guy was hydroencephalitic, if that's the right word. There were no vans in those days. I was a kid. I remember them lifting his entire chair, rain or shine, into the back of a pick-up truck. That was my biggest fear: 'Please don't ride me around in the back of a pick-up truck.'

I lived at my Dad's house until I was 28, because I was in a wheelchair. I got into a wheelchair at 17 and just stayed there – there was no reason to leave.

WHAT HAPPENED WHEN YOU WERE 17?

I was a lifeguard. We left work to go chase girls. It was raining real hard and we slid off the road. The driver of the car was Crazy Cat Jones. Never get in the car with someone named Crazy. It's just one of those situations where you want to say, "Now what tipped it off that you might

have been in the wrong place? Mmmm, the driver named Crazy?" It was a '71 Pinto. The kind that blows up. It didn't blow up.

Afterward, I wasn't working out with a physical therapist on a daily basis. Not in south Georgia. No one told me, "First these muscles will return, and you'll gain a little strength here. We'll work on these." I just sat around my house and watched wrestling on TV. I completed my last year of high school from home. The doctors said that it was temporary. I'd be up and running around in no time at all. So I pushed off having to deal with it. I remember going to school, trying to get into college and the admissions officer says, "Oh, what's wrong with you?" and I said, 'I'm temporarily paralyzed.' She said, "You are? When did this happen?" I told her and she says, "That's two years ago. That doesn't sound too temporary to me."

There are these little kids at my apartment complex who are just like family. When Keena was about six – I had known his family for about six months – he kept saying, "Why can't you walk?" I tried to explain it to him, but he kept asking, "Why can't you walk?" 'I can't, I can't, I can't.' He got very quiet. He walked across the room and he looked at me and, just like you would do to a child, he clapped his hands together, held his arms out and said, "Come on. You can do it." I thought if there was ever a moment where God would step in and go "Okay, boom!" it would be then. I really felt like falling off the couch and doing something to walk towards him. It was such a moment of pure child hopes and dreams.

WHAT ABOUT ADULTS' MISGUIDED ATTEMPTS TO BE OF HELP?

There was this time on the elevator where I used to work. You know how when you get on the elevator, you walk in and turn around. But with a chair, you need such a circumference to turn around that often you can't. So, my back was to the numbers and I kept looking back to see where we were. There's only seven floors in the whole building. My floor was the seventh. I couldn't really miss. But there was still a couple of people on the elevator, so I kept looking back.

At some point I looked back and said, 'Is this the seventh floor?' And this woman said, "No. Now, this is the fifth floor. I'm going to get off here. The next time it stops, that'll be the sixth floor. You don't want to get off there. The next time it stops, that'll be the seventh floor. You'll want to get off there." I said, 'Thank you.' She was just trying to be nice.

Another time, a guy with a bible got on. And I just thought, 'Shoot.' We're easy targets, especially in more rural, church-oriented places. I just smelled it coming. So he said, as the door closed, "You know, God put you in that wheelchair." And I said, 'And I'm pretty pissed about it too.'

Here's another good one. A friend of mine and I went to see *Platoon* when it first came out. I never went to Vietnam. And bless the hearts of those who did. The movie is over and we're in the lobby. There's 150 people in there but I locked eyes with this one guy across the way and I knew. I said to my friend, 'Jay, that fellow's coming over here.' He looks at all the people and says, "Who?" I said, 'That guy right over there.' "What guy, Tommy?" 'Trust me. Just watch.' The guy walked right up to me and without saying a word put his hand on my shoulder, nodded his head and walked away. I didn't have the heart to say, 'I was in a Pinto!'

Guys in bars, especially drunk guys, will say, "Let me buy you a drink. Man, I couldn't do what you do, sitting in that wheelchair. I'd go crazy. I'd kill myself. I couldn't do that." 'Yes you could,' I tell them. 'Trust me, nobody asked me. It wasn't like someone said, "everybody that wants to be a paraplegic, line up here." You do what you have to do.'

Generally speaking, people think you're retarded. I was on a date one night and the waitress took my date's order and then says to her, "And what would he like?" This was ten years ago. And Beth, my date, said, "Why don't you ask him?!"

ON THE TOPIC OF SEX, DO PEOPLE MAKE ASSUMPTIONS ABOUT WHAT YOU CAN AND CANNOT DO?

Absolutely. I had a real situation with women for a long time. And my shrink said: "You have two problems Tom. One is that you think women will always leave you, because your mother died when you were seventeen. And the other problem is you like (casual sex) at every opportunity." And so I was sabotaging my own relationships to prove, 'See, I told you women would leave me.' Self-fulfilling prophecy.

IN TERMS OF IDENTITY, ARE YOU PART OF THAT COMMUNITY OUT THERE THAT IS INTO DISABILITY RIGHTS? DO YOU THINK OF YOURSELF AS DISABLED?

I was once asked, when they had a big thing at the Governor's Mansion or the courthouse, "Tommy, did you know they chained themselves down there and held up traffic and everything? Why weren't you down there?" I said, 'Because I work for a living and I just can't go down there and piss and moan about stuff.' I'm sure that they made changes that will benefit me but I'm just not one to go and chain myself to something. I mean, here I sit eating a cheeseburger. I was in Helen, Georgia yesterday, driving on the interstate. I'll go swimming before the day is over with. I slept until ten. I made some phone calls. I made a little money, booked some shows. I put on my own pants.

BUT DO YOU FEEL ANY KIND OF KINSHIP OR GROUP IDENTITY?

I don't. Even when I was at Warm Springs, which is a rehabilitation place. Everybody there seemed to want to piss and moan, "You know, I almost died." "I can't move nothing." "You know, I've been dead four times?" Let's just top each other, shall we? There was this hierarchy of who's more disabled or who's been through more pain.

WHAT'S WORSE, THE PHYSICAL BARRIERS OR PEOPLE'S ATTITUDES?

My next door neighbor, she doesn't know who I am or what it is I do. So I was gone one day to do a show and my ex-girlfriend was at my place. And the neighbor says, "So, where's your husband?" She always thought we were married. "He's at work." "At work? He works? He's in a wheelchair, woman. Are you crazy?"

TELL ME ABOUT WHAT YOU DO FOR A LIVING.

Laughing Matters has a workshop every week and has for ten years. I do comedy improv and teach classes. I taught a class Monday, did six shows yesterday. I'll perform Thursday and Saturday. I'm such a junkie for it. There's that creative process and you never run out of ideas. You only begin to think you run out of ideas. I was just telling the guys the other day, 'We will use and discard more good ideas in the next two hours than some people will have in a lifetime.' Even in warm-ups before the show, somebody will say something extremely funny and I will tell them, 'You just donated that

TOMMY FUTCH

to the improv Gods. It will not go on that stage.'

WHAT'S IT LIKE WHEN YOU GO BACK TO NASHVILLE?

In my little hometown, I'm still regarded as "that guy in a wheelchair who played football in high school. I don't know what he's doing now." I got to reinvent myself when I left. But the mentality in small towns is that if you leave, you just must be too good for them. You can't go home again. I remember going to a barbecue after I'd been in Atlanta for four or five years. I really felt that I belonged to my home town but that the things that I wanted to do were not there. I went home as much as I could. But I remember encountering, "Oh you're an Atlanta boy now."

WHAT WOULD YOU LIKE TO DO DIFFERENT?

I would dance more. I don't like doing things that I'm not good at. I love to dance but I don't like feeling like half a dancer. I only dance when I've had enough alcohol in me. That's when I can break through that barrier. I can go to a nudist resort and be buck-naked all day long, but I cannot dance in public unless I've had a few drinks. ♣

"NOWADAYS, IT'S VERY POPULAR TO HAVE EPIDURALS . . . AND I THINK IF I WAS A DIFFERENT PERSON, I WOULD GO THE PAIN-KILLER ROUTE. BUT I WAS DETERMINED TO EXPERIENCE WHERE MY BODY WOULD GO, PHYSICALLY. I'VE EXPERIENCED SO MUCH PHYSICAL PAIN IN MY LIFE THAT WAS NEGATIVE . . . TO EXPERIENCE PAIN THAT WAS POSITIVE WAS IMPORTANT."

CATHERINE HOWETT SMITH

Museum Administrator

Catherine Howett Smith is assistant director of the Michael C. Carlos Museum of Emory University. A polio-like virus severely weakened her legs as a child. She spent four years at this same university as a student, having to crawl up stairs on her hands and knees to get to her classes. Getting into buildings is much easier now, but she says she has never felt so handicapped in her life because parenting is so much more physical than she ever imagined.

I had a blissful childhood because I don't think I really knew for a long time that I was different. My parents didn't let me know I was different. And sometimes I thought that was cruel, because they expected me to do things all my sisters did and that other kids did – you know, physical chores. I don't think it really hit me until I was elementary school age, when I got teased. There is always the bully in the class. I remember this one girl, who was relentlessly cruel in making fun of my leg braces and the way I walked. I remember being panic stricken when we'd play the game Red Rover. You know, "Red rover, red rover, send so-and-so over." No one wanted to call me over.

They've always just told me that they believe I had a virus. They call it polyneuritis – unknown origin. Polio-like in its affect because it came and partially paralyzed, weakening my hands but mostly my legs. I remember going to a lot of hospitals and having a lot of tests. I think they told my parents that it could be muscular dystrophy. In the end it seemed that it wasn't degenerative; it seemed to have come, done damage, and left. My parents don't have any recollection of me being sick before

this happened. They just noticed one day that I wasn't walking correctly.

Growing up, I had three "healthy" sisters. When we were young I used to struggle with, 'Well, why was I the one?' My sisters were all beauty queens and all had boyfriends. I had boyfriends too, but it's just that I felt so different from them. As I've matured, I've seen my sisters' pain in a different way. I have a sister who's gone through a divorce. Each of my other sisters has struggled with different things in her life that I haven't had to struggle with. And I'm now just so aware that all the advantages they might have had as youngsters have balanced out in the end.

My doctors would say, "You could try walking without braces." When I would visit my orthopedic surgeon, I remember always talking about how much longer I would have to wear the braces. As a child, I always thought there was some endpoint. And eventually, after I had some surgery, I would be the captain of the cheerleaders.

I remember one conversation with my doctor. I said, 'When are we going to do whatever it takes to make this better?' And I remember feeling like he was talking to me in a way that probably should have come from my parents. He was not fit to have that conversation. But nobody else ever really had it with me. I think I just came to some understanding on my own that I was disabled.

As I approached my teenage years, appearing handicapped was definitely an issue for me. I think sometimes I struggled more than I should have because I was so vain. I didn't want to wear the paraphernalia of a handicapped person. Sometimes you just don't want to deal with people staring and asking you questions. At some point I must have come to my own understanding, maybe as a teenager, that this was my life and there wasn't some surgery that was going to make it all better. In some ways it's been easier since I've taken on the trappings of a handicapped person because people don't wonder so much. They don't necessarily always need to know what happened to me. If I have my braces on they think, "oh, she's handicapped." Whereas before, they would just look at me and wonder why I was walking that way.

But then I decided that I'd just beat this. I'd just do what it took. I wouldn't wear braces and I wouldn't use crutches. In fact, I went for many years not wearing leg braces. But it made for a difficult life. And I did that for way too many years. It was a learning process. I wear them now. When I was pregnant, I used forearm crutches and it was so much easier to get around during the day. But I couldn't overcome this pride or feeling that I could beat it. There is a certain strength and maturity in not having that attitude.

Do you think of yourself as disabled now?

That's such a complicated question. I had intellectual gifts. And I think I always had incredible self-confidence because of those. Physically, I didn't have that self-confidence. And I think that's why having my daughter Hannah was so profound because it was the first time I did something physical – the ultimate physical experience. I had such a sense of accomplishment when I did that because it was something physical and it was good. I know I didn't answer your question. My self-identity has always been very complicated. But for Hannah it's so simple; I'm just Mommy.

It was an interesting and cathartic experience to write all that negative scary stuff. And then, all of a sudden, my poetry started to be more uplifting and positive. I think if I sat down to write now, I wouldn't have those demons anymore. I'm not sure where they went. I've dealt with them in some way. I think the older you get, the more people you meet, the more you realize that everyone has a cross that they bear. But when you're a teenager, you look at the captain of the cheerleading squad, the model who has the boyfriends, and you think, 'She doesn't have a care in the world.' And of course she did, but when you are young you never saw that. The fact that I can't go up stairs is an inconvenience. Whereas, when I was younger it was this terrible awful thing that made me different.

Do you feel any kind of common bond with other people with disabilities?

Definitely. Sometimes when I see someone on the street, a stranger who is in a wheelchair or walking with a forearm crutch, I just want to go up and say, 'I know.' There's some knowledge there that you only share amongst that group – there's something about our society that puts you in some other group when you are not physically "normal". Our society puts so much emphasis on physicality. You could be Michelangelo, you could be Shakespeare, you could be Jesus, but if you aren't Cindy Crawford, you aren't normal.

I have often thought that my life would have been easier as a disabled male because of that physicality. As a young adult I had relationships with "normal" men. I seemed to be able to attract men that wanted to have relationships with me. And I got married to a wonderful man. It says a lot about those men who were able to overcome those roles that society puts us all in.

Did you ever have doubts about your ability to be a mother?

I think when I thought about being a mom, I approached it intellectually. That's where my self-confidence was. I read every book you could ever imagine about parenting. I know what Hannah's life will be like until she's grown up – what she'll eat, where she'll go to school. At some point in my pregnancy I thought I was ready for this. I'd read all the books. I knew everything I needed to know. And then, you're faced with something that's not intellectual at all. It's totally physical and emotional, and no amount of reading changes that. I think that's been a shock for me. I'm still struggling with it.

There's a lot of denial sometimes because you want your life to be what you think of as normal. But you can't have much denial in the face of a crying kid that needs her dinner and you've got to get her from point A to point B. You figure out how to do it real fast. Now that Hannah is bigger it's an issue of actually having the physical strength to lift her. Also, I have balance problems. Especially when I'm carrying something. I can't keep my balance when I'm holding her. I'll just topple over. So, I sometimes won't do it because of her safety. I think it's hardest when she's learning to walk and she's still clumsy and she falls down or she cries. I want to just scoop her up, but I can't. Sometimes I think, God, it would be easier if I was in a wheelchair. I could just wheel right over and get her.

I don't want Hannah to ever be embarrassed about me. I don't want to ever not be able to do anything for her, that she needs. And I don't want her to suffer in any ways that I suffered. But I know that I'll be a good parent.

DID YOUR DISABILITY EVER POSE TO BE AN OBSTACLE TO YOU GETTING YOUR EDUCATION?

In college I had a really hard time and there was a point at which I tried to work with people on campus to make my life a little easier. I met with a dean. I was telling her I had classes that I just couldn't get into. I was tired of going on my hands and knees having everyone staring at me. And my hands were always dirty. It was just awful. And I was tired of not taking advantage of certain extracurricular things because I couldn't get into a building. I was just getting more mature and more strong and I didn't want to deal with it anymore. I was a good student. I was Phi Beta Kappa, and dammit, I didn't want to crawl on my hands and knees to get into my class. The dean didn't offer any solutions. She certainly didn't offer to build an elevator or a ramp. She said, "Well, couldn't you wait outside the classroom until someone comes along and ask them to help you get into your classroom?" I just looked at her and said, 'No.' I didn't know what else to say because she really thought that handicapped people should stand on the street and ask for help and not have the right to get into the classroom on their own.

I think I started scheduling my classes, not according to what I wanted to take, but where I could get to. And I know I would have taken different classes. I would have majored in something different. But I was designing my curriculum based on first floor classrooms and buildings that were next to each other because I couldn't walk long distances.

WAS IT ALSO DIFFICULT TO PARTICIPATE IN THE SOCIAL ACTIVITIES ASSOCIATED WITH COLLEGE?

I was in a sorority, which I hated, but it seemed to me to be the normal thing to do. I wanted to do normal things. But I just felt so different from all these perfect sorority girls. They do this thing called rush where you basically interview people to see if you want them to be in your sorority. It's just a horrible thing. There was a young woman who came through rush who had cerebral palsy. And there was a tradition in the sorority where they would pair people up. If you were from the same part of the country, they'd pair you up to talk during these rush parties. Well, they paired me with this girl who had cerebral palsy. We had nothing in common. We were from different parts of the country, but these sorority officers thought, "oh, they're both handicapped, they'll have something to talk about." I knew full well that they were not going to let her in the sorority. Sometimes, I think I got in because my sisters were in that sorority. I think if I had just hobbled up there on my own, I would not have gotten in.

DOES THE STEREOTYPE ABOUT POLIO SURVIVORS BEING PERFECTIONISTS DESCRIBE YOURSELF?

I would not attempt to do anything unless it was perfect. My mother used to try to demand that I make a B or an A- because she thought that it would be so healthy for me to do something less than perfect. This is amateur psychology but, I believe that I thought that I had sort of used up my quota of failure. I believe I had always thought that this handicap was some colossal failure and I had kind of used up my allotment of being imperfect. And so everything else in my life had to be perfect. It's a difficult standard to achieve. I still struggle with it. ☙

"THIS IS A FATEFUL THING THAT HAPPENED. I HAVE NOT AS OF YET FELT BITTERNESS OR ASKED THE QUESTION, 'WHY ME?' HOWEVER, I'VE WOKEN UP MANY A TIME WITH A TEAR IN MY EYE."

CURTIS MAYFIELD

Songwriter, Producer, Founding Member of the Impressions

In the 1960s and '70s, Curtis Mayfield gave us hit songs like "Keep on pushing," "People get ready" and "Gypsy Woman". His inspirational songs became R & B pop standards. Dubbed the "gentle genius of soul," Mayfield's music has had a major influence on contemporary black music. In August of 1990, Mayfield's career was brought to an abrupt halt when a lighting scaffold fell on him during an outdoor concert in Brooklyn, New York. The steel structure broke several vertebrae, paralyzing him from the neck down.

I started singing at a very early age, about eight years old. My grandmother owned a church by the name of the Traveling Soul Spiritualist Church. And there were lots of kids there for the morning sessions and Bible class. We started a group that was known as the Northern Jubilee Singers. This was back in 1954. Jerry Butler was one of us, who incidently, was one of the lead singers that sang with a group known as the Impressions.

We turned professional in 1958 with a label known as Vee Jay Records out of Chicago. And our first recording, *Your Precious Love*, was a very large hit for us. I always say we came in on the cusp, simply because the Fats Dominos and the Sam Cookes and other people of that stature were still working on the road. We were still the young kids. So we got a chance to see the old and the new – 'we' being the new generation.

Our styling, more or less, was founded from the church because we did a lot of harmonies. We did finally come up with a song, known as *Gypsy Woman*, which did very well for us. We began to

tour quite a bit all over the country. The country became a neighborhood for us. I guess we put about 200,000 miles on our car annually. Many times we had to sleep in the car simply because of the segregation; people wouldn't allow us to stay in the hotels, even though we had the money. So we learned from each other and we made good friends. Name them, we knew them – from Brook Benton to people like Little Richard. All the big stars would hit the tours.

DO YOU STILL WORK ON SONGS IN YOUR HEAD, SONGS THAT YOU'D LIKE TO GET OUT?

Songs are like dreams. But they're also like good conversations. And every conversation that goes from heart to heart can become a song because there are many hook lines and many honest to goodness feelings that cross over when you converse with people. And of course, in spite of my condition, I still dream of songs. I still have hook lines and I still have melodies. The only difference is that I just have not brought them all together. Hopefully in the near future, with high-tech and voice activated computers, and with friends and people helping me, there may be new compositions coming. I have done a few recordings with Warner Brothers and I am about to record a new album, hopefully for Warner Brothers. So far, so good.[†]

Warner Brothers has been so nice to me over the years. There's a [tribute] album out called *All Men Are Brothers* where all the big artists – Bruce Springsteen, Whitney Houston, everybody – recorded one of my songs. It was just fantastic. It was like I died and woke up to find a wave of love from the people themselves. I never looked upon myself as being such a celebrity that I couldn't speak to fools as well as kings. Those rewards, fortunately, have come in my later years. It has been some 35 years that I've been in the business. What is the average longevity of the average artist? It's not too long. So there are still great chances for me. And if I don't act the fool, maybe I'll still be around, in spite of the odds.

IS FOOLING AROUND ON THE GUITAR AN INTEGRAL PART OF WRITING A SONG? DID YOU NEED TO HAVE A GUITAR IN YOUR HANDS TO WRITE?

Well, I slept with my guitar. My guitar was actually another part of me. And I'm sorry to say that I don't have it any more.

DID YOU HAVE ANY PREMONITION OF THE ACCIDENT HAPPENING?

Oh, no. How could I? Actually it wasn't even my time to go on stage. I was there to close the show. But it looked like rain and there were about 10,000 people out there. I was the closing act. And the promoter asked me, "Hey, would you go on early? The people are here to see you and it

---

[†] In the Fall of 1996, Curtis Mayfield released a solo CD called *New World Order* on a Warner Brothers label.

looks like it's going to rain." It was about ten o'clock, so I was happy to oblige. Shucks! Just riding those airplanes back and forth frightens you and makes you say, 'Okay, this is the last time, this is it.' But of course, having been around the stage all my life, hey, I was in the safest place on earth as far as I could see.

And when it happened, I never felt it. All I know is that I had walked three steps toward the stage, after having come up the ladder steps. My band was playing *Superfly*. I was just thinking about not forgetting my lyrics. Then the next thing I knew I was laid out on the floor on my back. My guitar was gone; my shoes were off. And my hands – they were in another place. My feet were in another place. I felt like a bug, you know? I didn't know until I looked about myself and saw myself sprawled out like a rag doll. I knew immediately that I was paralyzed. And I just tried to keep my eyes open in fear of if I closed them I would die.

And then it began to rain, big drops of rain. And the fellas, they found a large piece of plastic and they held it over me. Luckily I was right around the corner from Kings Hospital in Queens, New York.

Of course, you don't realize how serious it is. The first thing that sets in is pneumonia. And the next thing they had to do was cut a hole in my throat so I could breathe. Then, after I started getting well, that's when I find out that being paralyzed does not mean that you can't feel and you don't hurt.

ARE YOU A DIFFERENT PERSON NOW?

I'm the same person in mind of course. However, in body, it's impossible for me to be the same because I'm totally paralyzed. And through the complications of being a quadriplegic, many times, the body dictates to the mind, rather than just the opposite. I can't be as independent as I was used to being all my life. I know already that I am quite fortunate. It can always be worse. And of course having a family, a wife, children, having been able to save my money – I'm still home. Even after all this, I have still seen some success and have been blessed with so many friends in my business ... to find myself at the Grammies, to find myself honestly still earning money. You never know when it might turn over. But I dare not think of that. I try to work and do things that may continue to help me earn money so I don't have to depend upon family or someone to help me continue on. And you know, people don't have to do things for you.

I've been an independent man, I guess, since I was 12 or 13 years old. And of course I can't be that anymore, at least I can't be without the help of others. That is a drag. Just imagine yourself tied up like a mummy; all you can move is your head. I can say this: I've always been quite adaptable. But this is a lot to accept. ♣

CURTIS MAYFIELD

"I WAS AT MY AUNT'S HOUSE ONE DAY AND I SAW A BIG PICTURE OF DOLLY PARTON AND I SAID, 'WOW! WHO IS THAT LADY?' I'M HOPING TO BE A COUNTRY MUSIC SINGER WHEN I GROW UP. I'VE NEVER SEEN A COUNTRY SINGER THAT'S IN A WHEELCHAIR BEFORE."

EMILY SHAW

Sixth Grader

New Kids on the Block never did anything for Emily Shaw but when she heard country music everything changed. She's been writing country songs ever since. Now Emily's room is plastered with Dolly Parton posters and a bulging scrapbook is always within hand's reach. Born with spina bifida, Emily has had 15 surgeries in her 11 years. Raised as a poster child of sorts for Egelston Children's Hospital and the Spina Bifida Association of Georgia, Emily recently discovered the joy of giving to others. She raised $450 in a one-girl Swim-a-Thon for a local shelter for homeless families. Emily lives in a suburban ranch house with her mother and father and brother Patrick.

People that don't know me stare at me. They stare because they are not used to seeing people who have disabilities. I didn't pay attention to it when I was little. I didn't think anything of it when people stared at me. I thought they thought I was cute or something. Now I understand it more.

WHAT ABOUT THE KIDS IN YOUR SCHOOL, YOUR CLASSMATES?

They know me. They don't think anything of it. They just think I'm like everybody else ... but I don't get invited over as much as other people. I'm sitting there inviting people over to my house. They make fun of me because I'm in a wheelchair.

THEY DO?

Yeah, of course. Doesn't everybody? I went on a field trip to Washington, D.C. It was lots of fun. We went to the capitol; we went to the memorials. I didn't like the hotel part because I was with some people who were mean to me. They wrote a song about me and it wasn't a good song

either. They thought I was asleep but I heard it. I clapped at the end of the song. I said, 'I heard the whole thing.'

IS THERE NO ONE ELSE THAT USES A WHEELCHAIR IN YOUR SCHOOL?

No. None whatsoever. They try and accommodate for me, like put in ramps. But it's kind of weird because they have to do it for one person. I just spilled my drink. This is how clumsy I am. I don't like it when people try and help me. They think that I can't do what they can do, but I can carry things just fine on my own. I might spill it, but I can get it on my own.

Patrick, Emily's brother who is a year and a half older, comes into the kitchen to get an Italian ice. He comes over and sits down with us. Emily does not like him being there. A frown on her face turns fierce and she punches him in the arm. He is determined to stay. She is just as persistent in trying to make him feel unwelcome. Patrick is busy defending himself. When asked why his sister is mad at him, he says, "Emily always has to have the spotlight." That's who I am, *she says.* That's why I want to become a country singer. I like the attention.

WHY ARE YOU SO MAD AT YOUR BROTHER?

Because he's a bonehead.

Aloyce asks her son Patrick point blank, "Has it been positive or negative having a sister that's disabled? Or both? His answer is unequivocal, "Positive. Theme parks, all the way. You get to go to the front of the line." Aloyce thinks of another bonus, "We rent Emily out at Christmas time – for the parking places." Patrick admits that there are some negative aspects: "Having to do all this extra stuff that normally I wouldn't have to do … like getting her wheelchair out of the car. And getting her drinks and stuff." Emily, who has been listening nonplussed to their complaints, feigns dismay: I found out my family doesn't want me. On the next 'Oprah.'

HOW INDEPENDENT CAN YOU BE?

Emily turns to Patrick and insists: And you can get out while I'm talking about this. *She whispers in confidence,* I don't want to talk about the personal care issues. It's embarrassing.

DO YOU PICK OUT YOUR OWN CLOTHES?

Yeah. Well I try to, but my mom picks out all these nasty looking clothes.

Aloyce says, "The problem is that Emily can only wear certain things because of her personal care. So therefore she has to wear skirts or dresses or culottes and Emily would love to wear jeans. Plus, she's a little overweight." Emily rolls her eyes, I'm outta here now. *She starts to roll away.* Either you leave or I leave, *she says to her mother. Her mother leaves the room.*

WHAT DO YOU THINK WOULD BE DIFFERENT IF YOU DIDN'T HAVE A DISABILITY?

I wouldn't get as much attention I bet. And people wouldn't stare at me and I'd have more friends and boys would like me. A lot of changes. It would be a big change if I could walk. Left, right, left, right.

YOU'D LIKE TO HAVE A BOYFRIEND?

When I get to middle school I'm going to go hunting. ♣

"THE ONLY REASON I FEEL LIKE I HAVE A DIS-ABILITY IS BECAUSE THERE ARE SO MANY HEARING PEOPLE THAT KNOW NOTHING ABOUT DEAF CULTURE."

BO CLEMENTS

Interpreter Training Program Instructor and Deaf Community Advocate

Bo Clements grew up the only deaf child in a large family during a time when the use of gestures and sign language was discouraged. To this day, none of his family can sign. Bo lives simultaneously in two worlds: the deaf world and the hearing world. The former fulfills his social needs; the latter fulfills his economic needs. He works two part-time jobs, one at DeKalb College in Atlanta where he teaches American Sign Language (ASL) and Deaf Culture in the Interpreter Training Program, and the other at Special Audiences and Stagehands, Inc. where he coordinates interpreters for the visual and performing arts.

I'm from a hearing family. When I was growing up, I didn't know anything about sign language. When I was four and a half, I went to the Atlanta Speech School and they taught me how to read books and to lip read. I had to go to speech therapy to learn how to speak. If I said something wrong they would slap my face. But in the underground world of the Deaf, I learned how to sign. When I was eight or nine years old, we'd hide in the bus on the way to school and sign to each other. They used to slap our hands with rulers if we would use sign language. Not until we went into elementary school were we permitted to sign.

Most of my friends are deaf. We go out to parties and social events together. But the hearing world is the everyday world. I am fortunate because I can speak pretty well – not wonderful. But a lot of hearing people don't understand people who are culturally Deaf and what it's really like to not have the ability to speak. It's almost like you have to let them know, 'I'm here, I'm alive, I'm okay, I'm not any different.'

DO YOU SEE DEAFNESS AS A CULTURAL IDENTITY?

You used the term "deafness." I don't like that term. It just focuses on the physiological fact that someone does not have the ability to hear. Capital "D" Deaf means that you identify, 'I am Deaf and I am proud of it. I am one of the Deaf culture and the Deaf community.' We have our own identity, just like the African-American culture. Whereas later-deafened people don't really have a culture other than the hearing culture that they grew up with. Especially later-deafened adults – they're still upset because they miss their ability to hear, they're still in mourning. Those of us who were born deaf, we're very happy. We're not really missing anything.

IN THE DEAF COMMUNITY, IN THE DEAF WORLD, THERE IS A LOT OF PRIDE IN GROUP IDENTITY. WHY DO YOU THINK THAT IS AND WHY HASN'T THAT HAPPENED WITH PEOPLE WITH CEREBRAL PALSY OR PARAPLEGIA OR ANY OTHER DISABILITY GROUP?

Being Deaf is very much an invisible handicap. You see me and I look the same as you. You can't tell until I start communicating that there is a difference. But with cerebral palsy or people who are blind, you can see right off and there is an immediate judgment. You might feel a little reserved around them. Remember, we have Deaf colleges that teach pride, that teach how to have a high self-esteem and how to set goals and look at the future. When you go to a school that has a lot of Deaf people, there are role models.

I have my hearing family but I feel like I have the other family, my Deaf family. With my biological family I feel a little bit bored and isolated. The communication is very simplistic. Heck, I get with Deaf people and I can gossip and learn a lot about what's going on in the world. ♣

Bo Clements participated in the interview through a sign language interpreter.

BO CLEMENTS

"I'M IN THE POLITICAL LIFE. IF I MAKE PEOPLE ANGRY, I'M A CRIPPLE. I'M A SON-OF-A-BITCH CRIPPLE."

J.J. BIELLO

Cherokee County Commissioner

J.J. Biello used to be a police detective. He was known as a tough guy who kicked down doors. Yet he prided himself on his unique style of calling victims a year later to see how they were doing. In the lobby of the new county Justice Center he helped get built, commissioner Biello is greeted, joked with, and clearly loved by all those who walk by – the sheriff, local newspaper reporters, staff. His energy is mind-boggling, considering the fact that he endures excruciating pain in his shoulders twenty-four hours a day.

Most of the time, when officers are working, they have a sixth sense. This time I felt that maybe something wasn't right. I went in. It was a restaurant that was being robbed. As I opened the door I was shot immediately three times. He had a gun to a girl's head. I rushed him, took out a gun and shot him. In the struggle over the gun, just like you see on TV, I collapsed from all the bullets in my body. I went to get my gun. He started out the door. He stopped, turned around, came back, straddled me, put the gun in my face, smiled, and tried to shoot me in the face. I turned. It hit me in the neck, severed my spinal cord and vocal cord and hit my lung. It was a pretty bad shot.

People were running all over. Blood was squirting all over. And I'm saying to myself, 'Don't close your eyes or you will die.' Sometimes, I regret doing that. Sometimes I wish I had closed my eyes and I did die. There's so much pain, mentally and physically. I 'love' when these people come up and say, "Well, life is precious." Not when you're living a life of pain, it's not.

I'm paralyzed from the neck down. It's a C-4 spinal cord injury. I live a life of total pain. There

49

was nerve damage done by the bullet severing the nerves and spinal cord. It's 24 hours of pain a day. I've never slept more than two hours a night in the last nine years. I cannot do anything for myself. I have to have paid staff and family and friends to depend on. I'm really blessed with a very strong wife, who has been very dedicated to me, and two boys – two sons who have been through hell and back. I mean, seeing their dad as the kind of guy who builds his own home and then six months later being totally paralyzed, totally dependent.

What kind of man was I before this change in my life? I guess I wore two hats. I felt that I was a good father and a good husband – a real family guy. I didn't go to bars or anything like that. I had some good friends in the softball league. I was involved with the church. I was involved with my family mainly. The other hat I wore was that of detective. I was a hard-core detective in Atlanta. I was given "Officer of the Year" by the Jaycees in '84. I liked the job and got along real well with the public, which I felt was one of my strong points. I could communicate with anyone, from a doctorate's degree to a ghetto degree.

We try and remain a normal family. But it's obvious, because of me being in an electric wheelchair, that my wife has lost quite a bit. I can't do the physical things for my boys or my wife but we still try to function as normally as we can as a family. It's an adjustment when they have to help me get into the van and strap me in. Everything is a major production. But you adjust even though you don't like it. They adjust. They've stuck in there through the hardest times. But I know down deep inside it's very, very hard for them. And that's part of the mental pain that you go through. It's mental pain that, if you let your mind get away with it, will kill you.

I'll tell you when you know you're disabled. When you go into a store and people stop and stare. When people come up to you and say, "How . . . are . . you?" as if I have a mental disability too. And I don't mean that in a hateful way to people that do. I turn around and usually say, 'I'm fine. How the hell are you?' That usually opens up their eyes.

It's terrible when you're invited to a friend's house and you know you can't get in. But not only can't I get in, it means my family doesn't go either. And you're ostracized from some friendships and parties.

I've always had a hard life. I grew up in a working class family. Everything I got I worked for myself. No one gave me anything when I was married. I built a nice home. I did it on my back. I prefer it that way. But if I had it to do over? People have asked me, "Would you live your life over, barring the paralysis?" I say, 'Hell no. I would want to grow up as one of the Kennedys. I would want to grow up in Florida, chasing women on yachts!' ♣

"HOPEFULLY I CAN GET A MEDAL. IT'S ONE OF MY DREAMS."

SAUL MENDOSA

Paralympic Medalist, Track and Field

Saul Mendosa is fast. He races in a lightweight, custom-built, three-wheeled racing machine. On weekends he travels the country competing in wheelchair racing events. Mendosa earned a silver and two bronze medals in the 1988 Seoul Paralympic Games as a member of the Mexican Team. For the past year he has been living at the home of Barry Ewing, founder of Eagle Sportschairs. Having studied industrial science in Mexico, Mendosa now works at Ewing's small manufacturing company, which has taken wheelchair racing technology into the 21st century.

I am from Mexico City. When I was six months old I got polio. I got the vaccination but there was a big epidemic in the place I was born. Since a child I have been involved in wheelchair sports. When I was a teenager it was very hard for me to understand my problem. Later on, when I was in university, I understood that people were very proud of me. Because I used to visit all over the world [racing], the students at the university would ask me, "How was Japan?" "How was Europe?" I was somebody special there. Not special because of my disability – I was special because of what I had done for my country.

IS IT DIFFERENT FOR SOMEONE WHO WAS BORN – ALMOST BORN – WITH A DISABILITY TO RACE COMPETITIVELY THAN IT IS FOR ATHLETES WHO HAVE ACQUIRED THEIR DISABILITY?

It is different because when you get a disease when you are a child, you understand that you have to develop the abilities of other parts of your body. In that way it's more of a process. I guess that it is harder when you have an accident. From one day to another, you have to change your life. Sooner or later, anybody who uses a wheelchair has to begin that process.

IS THERE A DIFFERENCE BETWEEN MEXICO AND THE U.S. IN TERMS OF HOW YOU ARE TREATED AS SOMEONE WHO HAS A DISABILITY?

Here in the States, people are more open to disabilities. I've met a lot of people here and we go everywhere – we go dancing, we go to the bar, we go to work-out. In Mexico ... we have to work on the conscience. They think that physical disability also means that you have a mental disability.

WHAT ARE YOUR ASPIRATIONS? WHERE DO YOU FORESEE YOURSELF TEN YEARS FROM NOW?

Well, the first thing that I want to do is get a medal at the Paralympics in Atlanta because I am working for that. Later on, I would like to work with children with disabilities, to show them how they can handle their disabilities or even develop in sports. For every human being, sports are important because they make you feel much better inside and outside.

WHICH ARE MORE DIFFICULT, BARRIERS THAT ARE PHYSICAL, LIKE THERE NOT BEING A CURB CUT, OR ATTITUDINAL ONES, LIKE PEOPLE'S MISCONCEPTIONS?

People's attitudes. If I have a big sidewalk, I can control it with my hands and I can take my chair. I have developed my body in order to do that. Everything by my hands. But with my hands I cannot change the minds of the people. ♣

NOTE: Mendosa fulfilled his dream at the 1996 Paralympic Games in Atlanta winning a gold medal in the men's T52, 53 5,000 meter race.

SAUL MENDOSA

"I'VE HAD JUST AS HARD OF A TIME SUR-VIVING CANCER AS I DID FIGHTING IT."

STEVE DAVOL

Camp Counsellor

Steve Davol says living with cancer is about peaks and valleys. With frequent recurrences requiring chemotherapy, even a common cold that comes along is cause for worry. Dreaming about the future is not something he has allowed himself to do. Instead, he has gone from living day by day, to week by week, and now is working on living month by month.

The whole thing started 12 years ago. I had an accident. I was out snow sledding and hit a tree. I thought I broke my leg. They X-rayed it and said that I didn't break it but there was something the matter; I had bone cancer.

I started going through chemo and radiation therapy and was able to get over the cancer really well. About a year and a half later, it came back in my lungs. About four months later it came back again. With this type of cancer – Ewing Sarcoma – it comes back a lot. That's something that I'm constantly afraid of. I did eventually have to lose the leg where the original tumor was. They took my leg off right above the knee.

Chemo – it's a double-edged sword. When I was a young kid, I was more scared of having chemo than I was of having cancer. When you sit there and doctors talk to you about the chemo and the side-effects of it that stay with you for a lifetime, you don't think you're going to die of the cancer; you think you're going to die of the chemo. It's hard to be off the therapy because it's almost like a security blanket. I know it saved my life; I love it and I hate it. I don't really know anybody else that has gone through the same situation as I have this many times and is still around to talk about it.

DO YOU PERCEIVE OR IDENTIFY YOURSELF AS A PERSON WITH A DISABILITY?

Personally, I don't think I am because I can function quite normally. I can't do some of the things maybe I used to, but I can get out there in society and stimulate the economy if I'm allowed to. But now that everything is over, I'm a 25-year-old on Medicaid. The problem is that I now have a job where I'm making too much money and they're going to take that away from me. The system makes me seem handicapped to society. It's kind of a trap. If I couldn't get a job, I could just stay on medical insurance. But then I couldn't get any insurance to cover me. Because of a pre-existing condition, I'm stuck.

YOU WORK WITH PEOPLE THAT HAVE OR HAVE HAD CANCER. HOW DOES THAT AFFECT YOU?

I work at Camp Twin Lakes. It's a camp for children and adults who are medically challenged. I get to go out and have a blast at this camp and just do normal camping activities. I've always been involved with the 'cancer camp'. It's so nice to have an existence for a week where you're the norm and people without cancer are the people that are maybe a little different. But, this last week I had a friend pass away. I felt so bad just because of what I feel is my loss. And it happens every couple of months and you wonder when it's going to end. ♣

STEVE DAVOL

"I HAVE A STRONG FAITH IN GOD. AND I BELIEVE THAT HE IS THE ONE THAT BROUGHT ME THROUGH THIS."

SCOTT NOEL

Customer Service Representative

Scott Noel was paralyzed in a car wreck when a drunk driver ran a red light. He was fifteen at the time. Eleven years later he left home and moved to a new city by himself, not knowing for sure whether he could live independently. He now lives in an immaculate suburban apartment and commutes to a job where he feels his employer has gone the extra mile to accommodate him.

I got hurt when I was fifteen. Two friends and I were on our way home. We had gone to a small birthday gathering. A man who was drunk ran a red light and hit us. The impact made me turn in my seat and hit the side of my neck on the dashboard. It did not hurt. A lot of people automatically think you'd be in excrutiating pain but everything just went numb. I screamed for my friends to pull me out of the car. They wouldn't because they were afraid they might hurt me. I was afraid that the car was going to blow up. So they did pull me out. An ambulance took me to the hospital. They knew what it was automatically. I was quadriplegic – a C-5, C-6 incomplete.

My spinal cord was not completely severed. I've been very, very fortunate. And blessed – I have a strong religious belief about why I was able to get what I've gotten back. First, it was just sitting, then trying to get used to standing up. Then it went from one step in the parallel bars to walking back and forth. Then I started walking with the wheels and finally with a four-legged walker. Now, after all these years, I just started walking with crutches. I'm up to walking thirty minutes at one

time, which is pretty good for someone with a spinal cord injury.

I have an electric wheelchair so I can get around more easily. I drive. I have a converted van. At the shopping centers and grocery store that I go to, people are just amazed. I never would have imagined I'd be doing all this – living alone, cooking, cleaning, washing clothes, mopping floors. I have no attendant care at all. Sometimes I still have trouble with stiffness and spasticity, which is something that is common with a spinal cord injury.

HAS YOUR DISABILITY AFFECTED YOUR SOCIAL LIFE AT ALL?

A lot of people have come up to me and said, "I just wanted to meet you, because so many people know you and I see you everywhere." I don't mind going out to night clubs or parties. I'm not trying to brag but I'm very popular. I haven't had any trouble as far as dating goes.

IF YOU WERE OUT WITH FRIENDS AND SAW SOMEBODY GETTING INTO A CAR THAT OBVIOUSLY WAS DRUNK, WHAT WOULD YOU DO?

I would definitely try to stop them or talk to whomever they were with. And I've been places where people have had a couple of drinks and I said, 'Are you sure you're okay to be driving? Don't be out there driving. You see what happened to me. And it wasn't even my fault.' That really snaps people back and they say, "Hey, okay." And they let other people drive.

DOES WORKING FOR A SUCCESSFUL COMPANY LIKE COCA-COLA OFFER ANY ADDED ACCOMMODATION WHERE YOUR DISABILITY IS CONCERNED?

Working at Coca-Cola is very exciting because I never imagined that I would work for a major company like this one. There have been valuable benefits. The [wheel]chair that I use cost $9,000. They paid for all of it. They modified my computer and accommodated me with my hours, so that I could continue my therapy. It has been a great company to work for. ♣

SCOTT NOEL

CHUAN CHI

Healer

Chuan Chi lives in his father's house. Born in Taipei, he contracted polio at nine months of age. Twenty years later he had an operation in which metal rods were inserted in his back to correct his posture. Chi continues to have seizures and problems with his memory and peripheral vision. Chi left Taiwan in 1980 to join his parents, who own a restaurant supply business in Georgia. At 39, his parents do not allow him to go out alone.

The attitude toward someone who has polio or uses a wheelchair in my home country is very different. The non-native people that moved to Taiwan after 1949, they don't care what your disabilities are. They are very helpful. But the native Taiwanese might do rotten things to you if you appear to have a disability. There were kids that would tease me and insult me with words.

DO YOU HAVE GOALS OR DREAMS FOR YOUR LIFE?

[Chi's father answers] No, no, no. He never think about it. He just stay home or go out with us to eat. We don't want him to go anywhere because of his physical problem and his memory. The worst thing is his seizure. When it's raining, he have seizure a lot. Most time he lose consciousness and fall on the ground. And the eyes turn white, just like dead. I've taken him to English class since he come to the United States and I stopped that because he scared the students and teachers in the school. They call me and said, "He is dying."

DO YOU REMEMBER THAT CHI?

[Chi's father] No, no, he cannot remember that. He has a very short span of memory.

IS THERE ANYTHING THAT YOU ARE PROUD OF CHI?

When I was in Taiwan I learned acupuncture. My teacher was impressed with my skill. During my stay in the hospital I met somebody in the emergency room. She had liver disease. Everyday they used this long needle and drained the water out of her belly. She was in pain. I couldn't stand it. One day I asked her if I could try to help her. I asked her date of birth, time of birth, and year of birth. Then one night I used acupressure for a few hours. Sometime later I gave her two treatments with needles. Her enlarged stomach went away. She did not have any more pain. I am very proud of that. I would like to do that work again but there is no chance of it. This state does not allow for unlicensed acupuncturists. You must be a medical doctor.

DO YOU PLAN TO HAVE A FAMILY OF YOUR OWN SOMEDAY?

I still depend on my family to support me. I cannot be independent. I am very close to the church. I talk to my friends there and ask them to please let me know when I can be of help. I don't dare to think of a girlfriend. I have a disability and I don't want to give anybody trouble. ❧

CHUAN CHI

Chuan Chi spoke to us through Angela Chen, an interpreter. His father speaks English.

"RIDING A HORSE IS SOMETHING THAT GIVES ME AN IMMENSE FREEDOM. IN A [WHEEL]CHAIR, YOU HAVE A LOT OF BARRIERS ON THE GROUND. BUT YOU GET ON A HORSE AND NONE OF THOSE BARRIERS ARE THERE. THE HORSES ARE YOUR LEGS FOR YOU. AND THEY KNOW THAT."

LAUREN McDEVITT

Paralympic Medalist, Equestrian

Lauren McDevitt was ten when she experienced a muscle cramp in her thigh. She went to the school nurse to lay down. Within an hour, she lost all feeling and movement from her waist down. It has stayed that way. Now in her mid-twenties, she is working on a master's degree in therapeutic recreation. She captured a bronze medal at the 1996 Paralympic Games in dressage, a test of ability of rider and horse to communicate and work together through a series of complex moves.

I was 'injured' in May of my 4th grade year. When I went back for 5th grade, my classmates realized that I was the same person that I was before – I was just sitting down. They didn't treat me any differently.

I started riding two months later. My Mom teases and says, "They got you on and they have yet to get you off." The first time I got on the horse I needed four people to help me ride. A back rider rode behind me for support. I had two side walkers on either side for support. And I had somebody leading the horse. I was told, "You can obviously progress from this, but how far we're really not sure." That made me say, 'I'm going to really push the limit on this, as far as I'm physically able to go.' Four years later I was trotting, cantering and jumping small fences. And I was beating able-bodied participants at local shows and competitions. I was out to prove that I could go farther than people expected me to in the sport.

IS IT DIFFICULT FOR YOU TO STAY ON A HORSE DURING THE DRESSAGE TEST?

No, not if I have the right kind of horse and he's trained properly. But instead of having an adaptive saddle to add to my stability when I ride, I hope to ride in a dressage saddle, like everybody else, someday.

Dressage is basically about being judged on a test. The test involves certain movements of the horse – different kinds of walks, different kinds of trots and halts, which involves moving in different geometric shapes around the ring. It's all combined into what they call a dressage test. The judge is looking at the horse and the rider's ability to make the horse look the way they should on the test. They're looking at the horse's movement, how the horse behaves, how they obey – basically, how nicely they move. You get scores on different elements of that test.

TYPICALLY THE WAY ONE CONTROLS A HORSE IS THROUGH THE LEGS, THROUGH THE KNEES, THE CALVES AND THE ANKLES. HOW IS IT THAT YOU ARE ABLE TO DO THAT?

My aids are through my seat and through my reins, and some with my voice. You have to retrain a horse to learn those aids. Horses are trained to respond to the leg. You re-teach them how to respond to the seat. What I found is that the horse is much more responsive to your seat and your rein than to your leg. If you think about it, the horse doesn't have buttons on the side of their barrels or their bellies that make them go. That's something that we've created.

It takes a very special horse to do what I need to do. They need to have a very calm, quiet disposition. They have to have very smooth gaits. They have to be very intelligent because I have a lot that they need to learn to be able to work with me.

My mare that I just retired is so aware of what my abilities are and what my disability is that she's very careful with me. She's very different when I'm on her than when somebody else is on her. She is very careful not to spook at things. If she feels me come off-balance she will stop. When I'm on the ground she's very careful standing beside me. And Skip, my new horse, is picking up on these things too. I've noticed I've shifted off-balance a couple of times and he has slowed down or stopped. Horses have an amazing sixth sense.

WHAT IS THE MOST BOTHERSOME PREJUDICIAL BARRIER THAT YOU ENCOUNTER IN YOUR LIFE?

I run into people who stop me on the street and speak very slowly or very loudly because they think because I'm in a wheelchair that I have a mental disability. They do not expect that I can do the things that I do, or go to college or go to graduate school or have a job or do the things that I'm doing. It's a surprise to a lot of people. And it shouldn't be because I'm just the same as anybody else and I want the same things out of life as anybody else; I just may go about doing things a little differently. Disability is not a change of the person and it's not a change of the personality. And it's not a change of the mind; the mind is not affected at all. It's just a change of lifestyle. ♣

LAUREN McDEVITT

> "ULTIMATELY YOU LOOK AROUND AND REALIZE THAT EVERYBODY IS BROKEN. THEY JUST ARE NOT BROKEN AS VISIBLY AS I AM. THE REAL QUESTION OF LIFE IS NOT, 'WHY AM I BROKEN, WHY ME LORD?,' BUT, 'HOW AM I GOING TO GET STRONG IN THE BROKEN PLACES, LORD?' THE SEARCH FOR MEANING IS PART OF YOUR OWN HEALING."

MAX CLELAND

Former Georgia Secretary of State

Max Cleland came close to losing his life in the Vietnam War when he reached down to recover a dropped grenade. The explosion severed his right leg and hand, and mangled his left leg. He returned to face civilian life as a triple amputee. Cleland campaigned and was elected to the Georgia state senate. He needed others to haul him up to his first committee meeting because the mezzanine level of the 1889 state capitol building was inaccessible. One of the first things he did was introduce a bill to make public buildings accessible. In 1977, President Jimmy Carter appointed Cleland head of the U.S. Veterans Administration. He served as Georgia's Secretary of State from 1982 to 1995, when he resigned to run for the U.S. Senate.

I had a wonderful childhood, growing up as an only child in a neighborhood full of male children. They became, in effect, my brothers and playmates. They were all older than I was so I learned how to play sports and do things that children my age probably weren't normally challenged with. I was challenged early and often. They beat me at basketball and beat me at baseball. Therefore, when it came time to compete with my contemporaries, I was always, it seemed to me, a step ahead.

I think somewhere in my elementary school years I wanted to be somebody. I wanted to make my life count for something. I wanted to be outstanding. I think church had a lot to do with it. "Make your life count for something. Serve other people."

TELL ME ABOUT HAVING TO MAKE THE DECISION OF WHETHER OR NOT TO SERVE OTHERS BY GOING TO VIETNAM?

That was a very trying decision for me. At Stetson, in college, I was in ROTC in the early '60s. By my second or third year, it was pretty clear to me that I wanted to be a helicopter pilot. Then I ended up on the Washington semester program to see government in action. And that changed my life because I fell in love with public service. So I began looking around at graduate schools and ultimately was accepted at Emory.

After I got out, I had my two years of active duty that I had to fulfill. It was at that time, in the summer of 1965, that President Johnson made the ultimately fatal decision to build up the ground forces there in a very massive way. It was interesting to find out in the MacNamara book that six months after he proposed the massive build up to Johnson, he had second thoughts and within a year he thought the war was unwinnable. As I was quoted by the *New York Times* recently, 'I just wish he'd have told me.' It sure would have saved me the trouble when I volunteered in May of 1967 to go to Vietnam. It sure would have affected my viewpoint knowing that at that very moment, the secretary of defense thought the war unwinnable.

I volunteered for Vietnam in '67. I only had a two year commitment. I actually extended that commitment for the purpose of going to Vietnam. I was supposed to be discharged when I got back. I already had my orders in my pocket to come home. I had not only a few weeks left in Vietnam, but only a few weeks left in the Army, when I got blown up. Believe me, I have gone back over that ground mentally many, many, many thousands of times. You know, "Two roads diverge in a yellow wood, and sorry I could not travel both and be one traveler long I stood."

So I went. There I was, in uniform, a young officer, a trained paratrooper. When there's a shooting war going on, and you are in uniform and an officer or a leader, there is a sense of obligation that you feel to be where the action is because that's what you're trained to do. That's who you are at that moment. So that's who I was at that moment: a young first lieutenant, paratrooper.

I arrived in Vietnam in June '67. And I was there for a year during the time of the big build up and the enemy attack at the Tet offensive and the siege of Khe Sanh. We had over 550,000 troops on the ground at that moment. The Siege at Khe Sanh was the longest siege of the war. It started in January 1968 in the middle of the monsoon season and didn't end until the week we broke the siege. I never shall forget that. When I got off that helicopter, I was scared to death. I was totally filled with terror. When I got off the chopper there on the landing zone overlooking Khe Sanh on our big helicopter assault, it looked like a valley of the moon. For about two clicks, which is 2,000 meters, it was total annihilation of every living thing. That's where the B-52s had dropped their 2,000 pound bombs.

Then we got rocketed the night of April 4th. We were hit with about forty Russian 122 millimeter rockets that night. I couldn't help but feel, thinking back, that the Russians, the Chinese and the North Vietnamese were all trying to kill me that night. I took it personally. Four young men were killed in their bunkers with a direct hit. God, I was sprayed with dirt and sand and everything else when those rockets hit, even though I was in the bottom of this crater. And digging fast to China. With all that and all the big build up about how strategic Khe Sanh was, bulldozers plowed over the airstrip within two weeks of the siege. How's that make you feel?

Then I was wounded on April 8th, technically the day that the siege was officially relieved. It's like coming up to this incredible moment and you live through the moment and you pay the

price and then boom. Life is different thereafter. And there's this Rubicon that you cross and things are totally different in your life from there on out. I was lucky to survive that. I was really lucky to wake up on the other side of the Rubicon, because you wouldn't have taken bets on me living through a grenade that goes off five inches away from you.

There was no heroism involved. I didn't know the grenade was live. I thought it came off my pack. It was just one of those freak accidents of war. I was medically evacuated pretty quickly. I couldn't talk because shrapnel had torn up my windpipe. I had a flak vest on though. That saved me from any internal chest wounds. But my right arm was blown off. My legs were blown off.

I was wounded on a hill just east of Khe Sanh. It was a clear day. Kipling, who served with the British forces in Indjah, captured that British Tommy view of life in his marvelous poem, *Mandalay*. And that is, that you are far away, in a strange land. The strange land does not really accept you and the people back home don't really accept the fact that you are there. But you're there. Kipling's writings are now some of my favorites because as a Vietnam veteran I feel much like one of those British colonial soldiers sent to fight in a far off foreign war. Kipling writes about a marvelous feeling he had in Burma. "On the road to Mandalay, where the flying fishes play. Where the sun comes up like thunder, out of China cross the bay." That morning of the 8th, the sun came up like thunder, out of the South China Sea. And little did I know that within a few hours I'd be 'med-evaced' to the South China Sea to a quonset hut where five doctors would operate on me for five hours and 41 pints of blood later I'd wake up with no right arm and no legs. And not only no legs, but no knees, which tremendously complicates the fitting of limbs, which is why I don't wear them now.

About a year later, that was when I hit bottom. That was when I hit my deepest depression. It was in the VA hospital in Washington at Walter Reed, which they called the "the snakepit." But the snakepit had a strong humorous side – plenty of black humor. Because you were in with your comrades and all of us were clinging to life, the group was the life raft. When one was down, the others would help pick him up. So the group therapy and group identity helped out more than we ever knew. You're set apart as an amputee; it helped us get used to it.

Anyway, I was lucky to survive all that, but I came home to a very uncertain future. I laid there in the hospital and cried hot wet tears of despair not having the slightest idea what in the world I was ever going to do with my life or what was going to happen, or whether I'd get a job or whether a girl would ever look at me again or whether I'd be able to drive a car or whether I'd be able to do anything. I had only known one amputee and that was a guy who was a drunk in downtown Lithonia. And all he did was hold up the light post. He was a single arm amputee out of Korea. I wondered whether all amputees were like that. 'Do you have to become an alcoholic?' 'Do you have to just hang around town for people to feel sorry for you?' 'Is that the role people expect you to play?' That was the terrifying thing about it. I'd ask doctors and nurses, 'What can I expect?' "Oh, well, we're not sure." 'Great. Now give me another good reason to live for a day.'

People used to say, "Are you bitter?" I'd say, 'No'. But you've got so much bitterness and hostility and frustration that you can't even articulate it. Which is one reason why, when I was head of the VA, I created the Vet Center Program. I knew all that anger and frustration out there was not being articulated and these kids were committing suicide and blowing each other away in peace time years later. It was called post-traumatic stress disorder, which really means a lot of emotional explosions going off in your life that you're not really aware of. So we created the Vet Center Program. That's the thing I'm most proud of. Now there are 200 Vet Centers around the country which help veterans and their families deal with the emotional aftermath of war. You've got to deal with it. It took me about 25 years to really get strong at the broken places.

WHAT ROLE DID YOUR FAITH PLAY IN YOUR RECOVERY AND YOUR MOVING ON?

I think it takes time for faith to work. One thing's for sure. You put shallow religion behind you real fast because it's not a shallow life you're are dealing with anymore. This is real gut stuff. You go through incredible emotions of peak experiences of "Oh my God, I am alive" to "Oh my God, look at what I've lost." And you vacillate back and forth between those emotions for years.

HAS YOUR DISABILITY AFFORDED YOU ANY ADVANTAGES IN THE POLITICAL ARENA?

I had an instinct for public service. I had that before I got wounded. But getting wounded gave me a new identity. I became a local war hero. I didn't feel like a local war hero. Now I understand what Jack Kennedy meant when they asked him, "How did you become a war hero?" and he said, "Simple. They sank my boat." I became a war hero because the grenade went off. I would have never had all these opportunities, quite frankly, had it not been for being wounded. I would have come back and been a frustrated history professor at a junior college somewhere. Probably would have been married and divorced twice and now acting out male menopause at 53 with a gold chain around my neck, an open collar, and driving a Jaguar. Instead, I'm a noble statesman and public servant, who wants to drive a Jaguar and wear a gold chain around my neck. ♣

"IN THE EARLY DAYS OF ADJUSTING TO HER BLINDNESS, MY DAUGHTER FIONA SAID, 'MAMA, I'M HANDICAPPED, LIKE YOU.' I SAID, 'FIONA, I'VE ALWAYS TOLD YOU, I'M NOT HANDICAPPED. YOU DON'T MISS SOMETHING YOU NEVER HAD.'"

NANA TUCKER GRAHAM

Retired Business Woman

Nana Tucker Graham grew up in the south of Georgia. She was born with leg deformities and walked on her knees until she was 13, when she had her lower legs amputated. Despite the scholarship she'd won, her father did not approve of her going to college. But that didn't stop her from attending business college in the next town. To get there, she hitch-hiked. She and her husband Kenneth Graham ran a successful restaurant for many years in rural Ware County.

When I was 13 years old, I went to Atlanta and had my legs removed through the knee joints. Both of them. Two months later I went back to be fitted with two artificial limbs. They were going to measure me for crutches. I told them if I had to have crutches they could have the artificial legs back. They were going to measure me for crutches anyhow. I sat down on the floor and stretched out and wouldn't let them. The artificial leg man said, "Well, just wait. She'll come around." I didn't though. I wore my legs even though I had to have someone on each side of me to walk.

Before that I walked on my knees. And I climbed. I just did anything anyone else did. But I just couldn't walk upright. The kids never teased me about being crippled. I didn't know I was so different. I graduated from high school in 1930. I didn't have any way to get to Waycross to get to college. But I went ahead and signed up anyhow. My father had a car. He had two cars. He could have gotten me over there but he was determined that I wasn't going. And I was determined that I would.

NANA TUCKER GRAHAM & FIONA PAGE HOBBS

So, I rode the bus over there. But, after two or three weeks of not getting to school early enough, I stood out in front of the house to catch a ride to Waycross.

HOW DID YOU MEET YOUR HUSBAND?

Kenny heard about this girl selling tickets at the bus station that walked on artificial legs. He'd never heard of anyone like that. So curiosity got the best of him and he came in to see me. He had to pretend like he was going somewhere, so he asked for the schedule to Peoria, Illinois. That was his home. And I was as busy as I could be. There were two buses in and I didn't need to be up there talking to him. I could just tell by the looks of him, he just wanted to talk. After he got his schedule, he went and sat at the lunch counter. I got on the bus at six o'clock – so he didn't get to talk to me no more that day. He was in there the next day to see me. He found out I went home every day on the bus. He asked to take me home. I told him, 'No.' He'd go put a quarter in the juke box and play *If I Didn't Care*. All the bus drivers kidded me about it after they'd heard the song about fifty times. I could have killed him for playing that song to me. I guess it was a week before I rode home with him.

SO WHAT TURNED YOUR HEART AROUND?

Nothing turned my heart around. I just went along for the ride! I just thought I'd go with him a time or two and get rid of him. We went together from September to March. We married the 23rd of March, 1940. We celebrated our 50th anniversary in March and he died in October. ❧

NANA TUCKER GRAHM

74

"PEOPLE ARE MORE COMFORTABLE WITH ME IF I GET OUT THERE IN THE AUDIENCE BEFORE THE SHOW AND TALK TO THEM. THAT WAY THEY SEE THE CANE AND THEY GET OVER IT. THEY DON'T STAND THERE AND SAY, 'HOW DOES SHE DO HER HAIR?' 'WHO PICKS OUT HER CLOTHES?' WITHOUT HEARING A WORD I'M SAYING."

FIONA PAGE HOBBS

Professional Storyteller, Christa McAuliffe Fellowship Recipient

Fiona Page Hobbs experienced the classic hospital nightmare. Recuperating at home from a routine hernia repair, something went very wrong. As a result of extensive hemorrhaging, her heart collapsed. Oxygen deprivation during surgery caused permanent blindness. Only months earlier she had been named as Georgia's first recipient of the Christa McAuliffe Fellowship.

I can remember when I stepped out of the hospital. I walked out into the bright sunlight and I could feel the warmth of it. Riding along the highway I remember thinking, 'Well, I will just never see any of this again.' Of course I cried all the way home. I felt like someone had dropped me down in a barrel.

I taught school for 22 years and in 1987 was granted the Christa McAuliffe Fellowship to teach storytelling to 8th graders throughout the state. Several friends of mine called the Center for the Visually Impaired and said, "This woman needs help. She's got a fellowship to teach and her life's on hold. Can she get into school tomorrow?"

I really envisioned being able to go back and teach. I envisioned a seeing eye dog, going to school to learn Braille. When I went to the Center I was still only four months into recovery. I got tired a lot; I couldn't last a whole day at school. And Braille was very hard for me because I had done a lot of sewing in my lifetime and my fingerpads were very tough.

The rehab teacher came out to the house. She told me to walk with my hands in front of my face and in front of my groin. And I said, 'My what?! Have I got to do this all my life?' And she said, "Yes. And you can't go barefooted because you might step on something that will hurt you. And you cannot carry something hot. And I'll teach you how to sort your socks." And I said, 'Bull, I'm not living like this.' She said, "You're not accepting your blindness, Fiona." Then she recommended a psychiatrist.

I will admit that I was in denial when I was first blind. I avoided blind people. I had known one blind person in my lifetime and she was very pitiful looking. She was our neighbor. Sweet, an immaculate housekeeper, but I remember how she looked. And I didn't want to look like that.

My Braille teacher had been blind since birth. She was very stern. I asked her, 'How do I manage? You know I have lots of earrings and necklaces and scarves and hats. I love clothes.' And she said, "Well, you just get rid of all those things." I said, 'Well, how do you do it?' She said, "I have a pair of gold earrings and a pair of silver earrings. I have a Brailled box that says 'gold.' The other one says 'silver.' And I have a pair of pearls." She had advanced to pearls. And I thought, 'Wow, three whole pair of earrings. I can't live like that!'

Finally I got this cute, neat teacher and she said, "What do you want to do?" I said, 'I want to go dancing. I love to dance. Do you think I'll ever be able to dance again?' And she said, "Yes, you can dance again." She called Studebakers and she arranged for me to go there in the afternoon. I had my folding cane. The bartender came up and asked, "Is that a collapsible pool cue? You a pool hustler?" This same teacher took me to Rich's and had them teach me how to apply my makeup.

I don't look blind. People forget, especially family, that I can't see. Having a mother with a disability, I have overcompensated all my life, just like she did. I'm a driven person too. It's very tiring. It's been my nature to always say, 'Oh, don't worry. I can do it.' And the fact that I look like I can see, there is no visual reminder I can't. ♣

"GENETICALLY, I WASN'T GIVEN A CERTAIN BODY TYPE OR A CER-
TAIN AMOUNT OF SPEED. I REALLY HAD TO WORK AT IT. THAT'S
WHAT I DREW FROM WHEN I WAS IN REHAB – JUST REMEMBER-
ING THAT IF I WORKED HARDER THAN EVERYBODY ELSE IN THIS
CENTER, I WOULD GO HOME SOONER THAN THEM."

ANN CODY

Paralmpic Medalist, Track and Field; 1996 Paralympic Games Venue Planning Manager

*Ann Cody was a high school junior enjoying the volleyball season when she caught
an upper respiratory infection. She awoke in the middle of the night in excruciating pain. The infection that moved through her did a lot of destruction. In a matter of hours paralysis had set in. She was later diagnosed with acute transverse
myelitis. Cody's passion for athletic competition led her to Seoul in 1988, as part
of both the U.S. Olympic and Paralympic Teams. At the Paralympic Games, she
won four silver medals in track and field.*

Ever since I can remember, I loved watching the Olympic Games. I started participating in
organized sports around the age of ten. I was always out playing and running. That just seemed to
be where I was happiest. I played varsity sports in high school and had aspirations of competing at
the collegiate level. So when I acquired my disability at sixteen, I thought all those opportunities
were gone.

It wasn't until 1984, about five years after I had acquired my disability, that the first exhibition
Olympic event for athletes with disabilities took place at the Games in Los Angeles. So I trained
very hard, made a lot of personal sacrifices, and made it to the U.S. Trials in 1988. I placed third at
the Trials, which qualified me for the Olympic Trials internationally. I then placed sixth and went
to Seoul for the Olympic Games.

After having this image your whole life of what it's like to be there at the Olympics, I was somewhat disappointed because our event [the 800 meter track event for women wheelchair athletes]

was not a full medal sport. We were treated as exhibition event athletes. We weren't housed with the rest of the U.S. Team. I felt like I was a guest. I was in that Stadium – the Stadium that was full of people there to watch Carl Lewis or Jackie Joyner-Kersee. But when I have gone to compete in the Paralympic Games, the spectators were there to watch elite athletes with disabilities compete. You're not there as a guest, you're the focal point of the whole experience. It's much more of a family. Paralympic athletes have such a natural bond because we all respect and recognize each other for more than our athletic ability.

WHAT'S THE MOST DIFFICULT THING ABOUT LIVING WITH YOUR DISABILITY?

Probably the thing that is most frustrating is that not everybody around me perceives me the same way I perceive me. See, I know what all my challenges are in my life – emotionally, professionally, socially, relationship-wise and everything. All of those things are part of who I am. And my disability is just one cubicle, one cubby-hole of that. So it's frustrating because I have to recognize that, when I meet people and when I'm trying to establish relationships or friendships, the disability is always in the forefront of their mind. ♣

ANN CODY

"IN REALITY, IT'S NOT A BIG DEAL. I MEAN, ALL I CAN'T DO IS CLAP."

MIKE MOORE

Carpenter, *Single-Handedly Woodworks*

Mike Moore builds things for a living. His material – heart pine lumber – is salvaged from old barns and abandoned tenant houses, which are as common on the Georgia landscape as the kudzu that envelops them. Moore was in his early forties when his local doctor misdiagnosed a fast growing sarcoma on his shoulder blade as a ruptured muscle. Seven months later he underwent surgery which left him with only one arm.

How did I get started making coffins? By the grandmother of invention: necessity. I was a peach grower for 17 years and worked the Knox family farm. They're an extremely wealthy family in this area. You've probably heard of National Homes, the pre-fab housing? That was Mr. Pete's business. He's been a big old timber baron for years.

Two summers ago, at 3:30 in the morning, I got a telephone call from Boone Knox, one of his sons who lives here in town. Boone said, "You busy tomorrow?" I said, 'No Boone, not particularly. Why?' "Daddy died and we need a coffin. You ever built one?" I said, 'No Boone, I hadn't, but hell, I guess I can.'

We hung up and I'm thinking, where in the hell can I get the dimensions of a coffin. It was about a quarter to four in the morning and I'm walking around the house thinking, 'Damn, I'm going to go back to bed. I can deal with this in the morning.' Next thing I knew, these headlights appeared. The family was ready to get the coffin built. They came in the house and I said, 'Well, do you want this thing with a rounded top? Do you want this thing as a tapered, traditional looking coffin?'

"No. We don't have time for that. We're going to bury him tomorrow." Well, one of them laid down on the damn floor and the others got the tape and they started measuring him! We came up with the dimensions of the coffin by measuring the son. I got to work and by ten o'clock that morning we had a coffin made. Honest to God, it looked like a shipping crate. I sent a bag of screws and an electric screwdriver to the funeral home. They loved the simplicity of it. I mean, this was a man that could have been buried in a golden coffin.

I was talking to a guy at the Blues Festival two years ago and he said, "You know my uncle had his coffin made when he was young and he used it for a book case." And I thought, 'Ah-hah! That's it.' So I started making coffins as book cases and selling them.

Eleven years ago I learned I had Hodgkins – came out of the blue. I did radiation treatment and it was gone. Five years later, a tumor turned up on my shoulder blade which, for seven months, my friendly local doctor kept telling me was a ruptured muscle. It turned out not to be a ruptured muscle. I called my father, who is a neuro-surgeon in Atlanta, and I said, 'They just told me I have a damn lump in my back that needs to come out now. I want some good doctors, quick.' He came down and we went to Augusta. They kept saying, "Fore quarter, fore quarter." And I'm thinking, 'Fore quarter, okay, that's okay. What else?' "Oh that's all, just a fore quarter." It didn't dawn on me for the longest time. I was walking in-between some of those medical buildings and I said, 'Tell me Dad, what all is entailed in a fore quarter?' He said, "Well, they take off your whole scapula, your whole shoulder and arm."

'Ah.' My mouth dropped open. They seemed to be in a big hurry. I had some kind of fast growing sarcoma. So they whacked it off. It's much worse in here [points to his head]. That's where it is the scariest and the darkest. In reality, it's no big deal. I mean, all I can't do is clap. And I must confess, the only other time that I consciously, really wish I had my other arm is when I'm hugging somebody. I just wish I had my damn other hand sometimes.

I think humor is the best medicine of all. If you can't laugh at it, you're really in trouble. And it's hard not to laugh when I go in the kitchen, buttering a piece of toast, nobody in the house but me and find myself holding the damn English muffin with my foot. I'm looking around making sure nobody's looking at me. How do you not laugh at yourself when you know you're holding your breakfast with your foot?

Right after I got my arm taken off, I said to myself, 'Think about all the things I can or can't do anymore. I guess motorcycling is out of the question.' I said, 'I guess I can still swim.' And my brother Bill said, "Yeah, you can still swim. As long as you can find a round pool."

My grand conclusion for this year is that the ultimate joy in this life must be raising your kids. My two children are the joy of my life. And see, my wife had left three months before this ordeal. I was married for fifteen years. We lived together for seventeen. She just 'nutted up' and left. She left me the children which was fine. I told her over my dead body would she take them. I've raised both my boys and they're wonderful. What satisfaction. I know everybody doesn't 'luck up' like that.

Do you consider yourself disabled?

Not hardly. I think I'm far more able-bodied than a lot of people. I just had this argument with a stewardess on a plane. A friend and I went to Galveston to visit another friend who lives down there. We got on the plane and I sat in the emergency exit row, because of course there's a lot more leg room there. And this youngster came up to me and said, "I'm sorry, you can't sit here." And I said, 'Why not?' She said, "Well, the rules say you have to be willing to help evacuate people." And I said, 'Of course I am.' Then it dawned on me! I said, 'Wait a minute. You're trying to tell me that because I have one arm, you don't think I can open this damn door and help people out?' She said, "I'm sorry. That's what the rules say." I said, 'Well, screw the rules. I'm sorry too. If you can find me a seat with as much leg room, I'll move for you.' She said, "Oh please don't do this." I said, 'Honey, I'm not moving. I'm more able-bodied than anybody on this damn plane.'

So she went and got her supervisor, who was this great chief stewardess I suppose. I really liked her. It was like talking to Whoopi Goldberg with an accent. She said, "Man, you ain't going to give me no hard time, are you now?" I said, 'No, just find me a seat with this much leg room.' She put me in first class with my own little private booth. It was great.

Now I suppose that the rest of the world considers me more disabled than I do. But the social security administration doesn't consider me disabled. I went and asked them and they said, "I'm sorry. The book says that you have to be missing either your leg above the knee or you have to be missing two limbs." I said, 'Well, how about a hand, an elbow, a shoulder, and a forearm? How about that?' "Oh no. That doesn't fit. That's not what the book says." So if the government can't consider me disabled I sure as hell can't either. ♣

"IF I EVER WRITE MY AUTOBIOGRAPHY, I'M GOING TO TITLE IT: 'I WAS BORN COLORED AND CRIPPLED BUT NOW I'M BLACK AND DISABLED.'"

KATE GAINER

Disability Affairs Coordinator for the City of Atlanta

Kate Gainer was one of 18 students to attend Atlanta's first special education class for black children. It was an empowering experience for a black child growing up in a Southern segregated city. She says the most frustrating thing she went through as a teenager with cerebral palsy was that she couldn't "strut" like the other girls could. Gainer's intelligence, spunk and warmth has made her an invaluable advocate for people with a disability.

I t [special education in Atlanta] began during segregation. There was white special ed. and then there was black special ed. During that time the Caucasian special ed. was found mainly in private schools, set up by parents of kids with a disability. Then the Easter Seals Society decided to start a class for black kids. That was 1953. It was an interesting class in that it was a first. The teacher brought an added ingredient that they could not have found in most other people. She 'adopted' all 18 of us, meaning that she wanted the best for her 'babies'. She also challenged us to be the best we could be. She didn't set limits for us. She always talked in terms of me going to college. And back then that was highly unusual. You were lucky if you got to high school. But she'd say, "When Kate goes to college," rather than, "If Kate goes to college." And my parents were the same way. My whole extended family was that way. They exposed me to anything and everything they could.

I somehow escaped the harsher sides of segregation but I remember being very aware of it. Like when I went to see the doctor at Emory University. We all went to the same clinic, three times a year. The white kids sat on one side and the black kids sat on the other. There was a line down the middle of the floor. But kids being kids, gather on the line and play, in spite of the adults.

One day my uncle told me, "Kate, you won't be able to run and play with the other kids, but I'm going to teach you things that you can share." So he taught me how to play checkers, he taught me how to play cards, he taught me how to shoot dice and he told me dirty jokes – all those devilish things that kids love. But they were things I could share with the neighborhood kids whom were always encouraged to come to my house. I was never left out.

During my teenage years, the most frustrating thing I went through as a person with cerebral palsy was that I couldn't strut like the other girls could. I couldn't flirt with my body because I wore braces. I didn't have a particularly good body – I looked like a stick. All the 'movements' associated with cerebral palsy kept my weight down. I weighed 95 pounds all of my teenage years. I was straight up and down. And I could've just killed my sister; she always had the hourglass figure. So I had to learn to flirt with my brain.

Dates were non-existent, which was another frustration. I was interested in boys, of course – came out of the womb interested in boys. As long as we were kids, boys were interested in me. Or, if they had a disability too it was okay. But boys who were able-bodied weren't interested. I think it was the mind-set about disability at the time, but it was also a black thing. Because black men had so much going against them, they at least needed their woman to be an asset. And they didn't view me as an asset. So I was stuck. I was friends with a lot of them though. They would try their pick-up lines out on me to see how girls would react to them.

YOU HAVE A FAMILY, RIGHT? YOU DIDN'T STAY STUCK. SO WHAT HAPPENED?

I grew up. I went to Warm Springs. That was where I lost my virginity. I say I gave it away – gladly gave it away; it was a real burden to me. I think it is for a lot of people with disabilities. Especially so during those days when you were expected to be a virgin until you got married. But what happened if you didn't get married? Are you supposed to completely miss that side of life?

My first experience was clumsy. He was clumsy. I was clumsy. I remember saying, 'never again.' I think we've all had one of those at one time or another. But then I fell in love with this guy and he loved me. He was very protective and very secure within himself. All that good stuff. We had a good relationship for four years.

When I announced that I was engaged, my mother said "no way". He was blind. Even though my mother has always been my best advocate, and still is in many ways, in that way, she wasn't supportive. When I came home for a weekend with my birth control pills, she wasn't ready for that. She really wasn't ready for me to grow up.

ON THE SUBJECT OF MOTHERS AND LETTING GO OF CHILDREN, DO YOU THINK THAT IT IS HARDER FOR MOTHERS OF A CHILD WITH A DISABILITY?

Yes, especially if they're still the caretaker. It's hard to see a son or a daughter as an adult if you're still wiping his face or giving her a bath every morning. It's hard to change roles. And even though my mother didn't have to do those things for me any longer, her maternalism was still more pronounced. It was always expected that I would be passed down. My parents expected that I would live with them until they died and then I'd be passed down to my sister. My sister was ready to take that on but I wasn't consulted. I always expected to have a life of my own.

WHAT DO YOU THINK ARE SOME OF THE STEREOTYPES THAT RUN THROUGH A PERSON'S MIND WHEN THEY SEE YOU?

It depends on what I am doing at the time. When I was walking, the first reaction was, "WHAT?" My 'movements' would be going and I'd be concentrating so hard on balancing myself that my personality never really would come through. If I happened to be in a store, they were afraid that I'd knock down the merchandise! But now that I use my wheelchair, the first thing they see is the chair. And most are curious about that, especially because it's a power chair. Kids are fascinated. And I love kids.

Adults sit and stare, which is okay. It's natural to stare at something that's different or unusual. And unfortunately, we are still different and unusual. But beyond that, hopefully they see someone who is going about her life the best way that she can. As always, the biggest obstacle is the attitudes.

HOW DO YOU RELATE WITH OTHER PEOPLE WITH A DISABILITY?

I think I am more at peace with other people with disabilities. I can relax a little. I don't have to "be all you can be." I think some of us are more accepting of each other. We accept the differences and move on to other more important things about the person.

There are times when I really prefer to be with people with disabilities. There are common intrinsic qualities within all of us, whether our disability was acquired or something we were born with. I think there is an acknowledgment, "Hey you're one of us. Welcome." People without disabilities wouldn't necessarily understand that welcome.

But cerebral palsy (CP) is a very different disability. I tell my friends that have CP that we have a disability that is not socially acceptable yet. People don't understand the movements. Because of the movements, the facial expressions and the sound of our voices, people think of mental retardation. Some of us do have mental retardation, but because you have CP doesn't mean you have mental retardation. I say, 'accept me'. I've accepted myself. I've dealt with it. I had no other choice.

YOU HAVE A TEENAGER. IS THAT HARD?

It's hard because he's a teenager and because he's a boy ... and because he's a black man ... and because of the way society is now. Momma doesn't know anything. Daddy can be tolerated; Momma can't. And because Mommy and Daddy are divorced now, it's even harder. He wants us together.

He's always been my best defender, even as a baby. He's always been proud of Momma. When he was seven years old he asked me for a wheelchair for Christmas. When I explained to him that he didn't need one, he still wanted one. I was involved with a wheelchair soccer team and wanted him to play the game in his own local league. He wouldn't because they didn't use wheelchairs. He didn't see any sense in running around when you could roll.

His generation is the first generation that had the unique opportunity to have people with disabilities as heroes. He adored some of the guys that I played soccer with. He wanted to be just like them, to my chagrin. They were all womanizers. ♣

SELECTED RESOURCES

A WHOLE NEW LIFE, by Reynolds Price, New York: MacMillan Publishing, 1994.

ALICE IN BED, a novel by Cathleen Schine. New York: Alfred Knopf, 1983.

"ARE YOU RETARDED?" "NO, I'M CATHOLIC.": QUALITATIVE METHODS IN THE STUDY OF PEOPLE WITH SEVERE HANDICAPS, by P.A. Adler and P. Adler, Qualitative Research Methods Series, Vol. 6, Newbury Park, CA: Sage, 1987.

DEAF HERITAGE: A NARRATIVE HISTORY OF DEAF AMERICA, by Jack R. Gannon, Silver Spring, MD: National Association of the Deaf, 1981.

DEAF IN AMERICA: VOICES FROM A CULTURE, by Carol Paddon and Tom Humphries, Cambridge, MA: Harvard University Press, 1988.

DESPITE THIS FLESH: THE DISABLED IN STORIES AND POEMS, edited by Vassar Miller, Austin: Texas University Press, 1985.

THE DISABLED STATE, by Deborah Stone, Philadelphia: Temple University Press, 1984.

DON'T WORRY, HE WON'T GET FAR ON FOOT: THE AUTOBIOGRAPHY OF A DANGEROUS MAN, by John Callahan, New York: Vintage, 1989.

FDR'S SPLENDID DECEPTION, by Hugh Gregory Gallagher: Vandemere, 1994.

FOR HEARING PEOPLE ONLY: ANSWERS TO SOME OF THE MOST COMMONLY ASKED QUESTIONS ABOUT THE DEAF COMMUNITY, ITS CULTURE, AND THE "DEAF REALITY", by Matthew S. Moore and Linda Levitan, Rochester: Deaf Life Press, 1993.

FREAK SHOW: PRESENTING HUMAN ODDITIES FOR AMUSEMENT AND PROFIT, by R. Bogdan, Chicago: University of Chicago Press, 1988.

HOW IT FEELS TO LIVE WITH A PHYSICAL DISABILITY, by Jill Krementz, New York: Simon & Shuster, 1992.

IMAGES OF THE DISABLED, DISABLING IMAGES, edited by Alan Gartner and Tom Joe: Praeger, 1986.

INTERPRETING DISABILITY: A QUALITATIVE READER, edited by Philip M., Dianne L. Ferguson, and Steven J. Taylor, New York: Teachers College Press, 1992.

THE MAKING OF BLIND MEN, by R. Scott, New York: Russell Sage Foundation, 1969.

MISSING PIECES: A CHRONICLE OF LIVING WITH A DISABILITY, by Irving Kenneth Zola, Philadelphia: Temple University Press, 1982.

MOVING VIOLATIONS: WAR ZONES, WHEELCHAIRS AND DECLARATIONS OF INDEPENDENCE, by John Hockenberry, New York: Hyperion, 1995.

NO PITY: PEOPLE WITH DISABILITIES FORGING A NEW CIVIL RIGHTS MOVEMENT, by Joseph Shapiro, New York: Times Books, 1993.

ORDINARY LIVES: VOICES OF DISABILITY AND DISEASE, edited by Irving Kenneth Zola, Cambridge, MA: Apple-wood Books, 1982.

ORDINARY MOMENTS: THE DISABLED EXPERIENCE, edited with photographs by Alan J. Brightman, Baltimore: University Park Press, 1984.

OUTSIDERS IN A HEARING WORLD: A SOCIOLOGY OF DEAFNESS, by P.C. Higgins, Beverly Hills, CA: Sage, 1980.
PAST DUE: A STORY OF DISABILITY, PREGNANCY AND BIRTH, by Anne Finger, Seal Press, 1990.

A PLACE OF THEIR OWN: CREATING THE DEAF COMMUNITY IN AMERICA, by John Van Cleve and Barry Crouch, Washington, D.C.: Gallaudet University Press, 1989.

THE PSYCHOLOGICAL & SOCIAL IMPACT OF DISABILITY, edited by Robert P. Marinelli and Arthur E. Dell Orto, third edition, New York: Springer Publishing Company, 1991.

SEEING VOICES: A JOURNEY INTO THE WORLD OF THE DEAF, by Oliver Sacks, Berkeley: University of California Press, 1989.

STIGMA: NOTES ON THE MANAGEMENT OF SPOILED IDENTITY, by Erving Goffman, Englewood Cliffs, NJ: Prentice-Hall, 1963.

STRONG AT THE BROKEN PLACES: A PERSONAL STORY, by Max Cleland, Atlanta: Cherokee Publishing Company, 1989.

THE UNEXPECTED MINORITY: HANDICAPPED CHILDREN IN AMERICA, by J. Gliedman and W. Roth, New York: Harcourt, Brace, & Jovanovich, 1980.

TRIUMPH OF THE HUMAN SPIRIT - THE COMMEMORATIVE BOOK OF THE 1996 PARALYMPIC GAMES, edited by Jeffrey Tiessen, Oakville, ON: Disability Today Publishing Group Inc., 1996.

"WHAT HAPPENED TO YOU?" WRITING BY DISABLED WOMEN, edited by Lois Keith, New York: New Press, 1996.

WITH WINGS: AN ANTHOLOGY OF LITERATURE BY AND ABOUT WOMEN WITH DISABILITIES, edited by Marsha Saxton and Florence Howe, New York: Feminist Press of the City University of New York, 1987.

WOMEN WITH DISABILITIES: ESSAYS IN PSYCHOLOGY, CULTURE, AND POLITICS, edited by Michelle Fine and Adrienne Asch, Philadelphia: Temple University Press, 1988.